# YOUR LIFEPATH

# YOUR LIFEPATH

*HOW TO MAKE EACH STAGE OF YOUR LIFE EXCEPTIONAL*

NEAL ENGSTROM

Copyright © 2024 by Neal Engstrom

All rights reserved.

Printed in the United States of America

First edition, 2024

No part of this publication may be reproduced, stored in a retrieval system, or transmitted in any form or by any means, electronic, mechanical, photocopying, recording, scanning, or otherwise, without the prior written permission of the publisher except in the case of brief quotations embodied in critical articles and reviews. For information, address Foothills Media Group, 701 N Brand Blvd., Suite 810, Glendale, CA 91203.

YOUR LIFEPATH may be purchased in bulk for promotional, educational or business use. Please contact your local bookseller or the Foothills Media Group sales department at business@FoothillsMG.com.

This publication contains the opinions and ideas of its author. It is intended to provide helpful and informative material on the subjects addressed in the publication. The author and publisher specifically disclaim all responsibility for any liability, loss or risk, personal or otherwise, which is incurred as a consequence, directly or indirectly, of the use and application of any of the contents of this book.

Publisher's Cataloging-in-Publication Data

Names: Engstrom, Neal, 1966- author.

Title: Your lifepath : how to make each stage of your life exceptional / Neal Engstrom.

| | |
|---|---|
| Description: | First edition. | Glendale, CA : Foothills Media Group, [2024] | Includes bibliographical references. |
| Identifiers: | ISBN: 979-8-9913382-1-9 (paperback) | 979-8-9913382-2-6 (ebook) | LCCN: 2024947131 |
| Subjects: | LCSH: Self-actualization (Psychology) | Self-evaluation. | Self-realization. | Success. | Motivation (Psychology) | Role models. | Goal (Psychology) | Maturation (Psychology) | Self-help techniques. | LCGFT: Self-help publications. | BISAC: SELF-HELP / Personal Growth / Success. | SELF-HELP / Motivational & Inspirational. | FAMILY & RELATIONSHIPS / Life Stages / General. |
| Classification: | LCC: BF637.S4 .E54 2024 | DDC: 158.1--dc23 |

ISBN: 979-8-9913382-1-9 (paperback)
ISBN: 979-8-9913382-2-6 (ebook)

*This book is for you.
A guide to pursuing fulfillment.
Take from it whatever you need.*

ADVENTURE > MISSION > FAMILY / LEGACY / TRIBE

# CONTENTS

## 1. HAVE ADVENTURES

| | | | |
|---|---|---|---|
| A Full Bag of Luck | 1 | A Collection of Winning Pieces | 21 |
| Confronting Dragons | 3 | You *Are* Your Behavior | 23 |
| Traveling Light | 5 | Refining Your Personal Code | 25 |
| Happiness vs. Fulfillment | 7 | Be Great, not Perfect | 27 |
| Cobble Together Successes | 9 | Make Others Feel Good | 29 |
| From Innocence to Experience | 11 | Volcanic Moments | 31 |
| Run Your Own Race | 13 | Training and Observation | 33 |
| We're in This Together | 15 | A Lion in the Shade | 35 |
| Seize Opportunity | 17 | Change the World? | 37 |
| Mentors "Pass Through" | 19 | Who am I? | 39 |

## 2. CHOOSE MISSION

| | | | |
|---|---|---|---|
| The Mission | 41 | Purposeful Addiction | 61 |
| Plan *Your* Mission | 43 | Extraordinarily Thick Skin | 63 |
| The Final Question | 45 | Life as a Wrestling Match | 65 |
| Mission Prototypes | 47 | Let the Mission Unfold | 67 |
| The Seductions of Laloki | 49 | You're a Professional | 69 |
| The Immortality Project | 51 | Keep the Momentum Going | 71 |
| Distractions Are "Termites" | 53 | The Ultimate Price | 73 |
| The Mission Is a Project | 55 | Shooting Stars | 75 |
| The Mission Is a Work of Art | 57 | The Mission Track | 77 |
| Create Your Own World | 59 | Beyond the Mission | 79 |

## 3. START FAMILY

| | | | |
|---|---|---|---|
| Stick Your Neck Out | 81 | Can You Teach? | 101 |
| A Complementary Mixture | 83 | Everything Is Amplified | 103 |
| Belong to Someone | 85 | Born Unempathetic | 105 |
| Ultimately, We're Builders | 87 | The Family Glue | 107 |
| Your In-Laws | 89 | Your Kids Aren't Your Mission | 109 |
| The Most Delightful People | 91 | I Can't Stop You | 111 |
| A Project with Your Kids | 93 | Dig Back Out | 113 |
| I'm Proud of You | 95 | Transcending Your Teachings | 115 |
| Extra Parents | 97 | No Questions Asked | 117 |
| Warts and Imperfections | 99 | Gratitude Across Generations | 119 |

## 4. LEAD TRIBE

| | | | |
|---|---|---|---|
| Tribes in Ancient Times | 121 | Collect Good People | 141 |
| The Tribal Chieftain | 123 | What Do You Stand For? | 143 |
| Leadership vs. Management | 125 | Someone They Could Trust | 145 |
| Under Your Protection | 127 | Scarcity = Conflict | 147 |
| The Allure of the Tribe | 129 | Questing for Resources | 149 |
| Distilling the Tribal Mission | 131 | Neutralize Competitors | 151 |
| Teach and Train Your People | 133 | Building an Alliance | 153 |
| Playing Without Restrictions | 135 | Difficult Decisions | 155 |
| Absorb Uncertainty | 137 | Tribes vs. Institutions | 157 |
| Tell Beautiful Stories | 139 | A Powerful Tribe | 159 |

## 5. LEAVE LEGACY

| | | | |
|---|---|---|---|
| Legacy Replaces Mission | 161 | What Is My Destiny? | 181 |
| Recluses & Oddballs | 163 | Life Cycle of the "Self" | 183 |
| Full Trophy Cases | 165 | Casting Away the Self | 185 |
| Passing the Torch | 167 | I Hand You My Dream | 187 |
| Five Forms of Legacy | 169 | Top-Five Bucket List | 189 |
| Wisdom of the Elders | 171 | Finding Oneness | 191 |
| Elegant and Unrushed | 173 | Grant Them Immortality | 193 |
| Legacy Provides Immortality | 175 | An Unknown Destination | 195 |
| Four Belief Systems | 177 | Who Will Miss Me? | 197 |
| A Spiritual Awakening | 179 | Rejoining the Source | 199 |

# 1. HAVE ADVENTURES

## A Full Bag of Luck

The bush plane's engine throbbed and roared, and seemed to want to tear its way out of the cowling. Low clouds and light rain had the two pilots hugging the Alaskan tundra, a yellowish-green mosquito-infested sponge, at just 700 feet. With the crunch of gravel and the skid of rubber they slid into the makeshift strip. The pilots walked over and handed a bag of supplies to a sobbing Inuit woman. Her husband had crashed a plane and been killed the day before. I, the younger pilot, who had only been in Alaska a short time, asked the older one if he had known the man who died. "Sure, I knew him," he said, twisting his mustache. "Look, rookie. Up here every new pilot starts out with a full bag of luck and an empty bag of experience. It's up to you to find a way to fill the bag of experience before the bag of luck runs out."

You may not be an aviator. But as a young adult who has just finished your schooling, the world considers you a rookie. So go out and gain experience. Explore new and exotic territory. Push yourself to do something exciting and scary and perhaps even hazardous. As a new adult there is no higher priority than finding out who you are and what you want out of life. Learning this is impossible without testing yourself through a series of adventures.

Work at a bush charter operation in Alaska. Hitchhike through Europe. Teach orphans in Calcutta. Become a whitewater rafting guide in Idaho. Try modeling in Paris. Be a roughneck on an oil rig in the Gulf of Mexico. Harvest grapes at a vineyard. Work for the Peace Corps in Africa. Trek through Nepal. Play semi-pro hockey in Canada. Join the crew of a yacht and circle the globe. Try your hand at entrepreneurship, and start a company on a shoestring. Bartend your way across Australia.

The opposite of adventure is safe routine—something there's too much of today. A person can go from high school to college to an entry-level job to graduate school and on to a specialized career without ever having left the school/work pipeline. In today's world we no longer have rights of passage that officially mark the beginning of adulthood as our forebears did in ancient tribal times.

Life today is too comfortable. Too secure. Often new adults have a rented apartment, a leased car, and an employer telling them what to do. All of that prevents them from obtaining the genuine experiences needed to feel truly alive. Do you want to go out with your own fishing pole and your own bait and wrestle a marlin into submission with your own hands? Or, do you want your boss to pat you on the back and hand you money for a fish dinner that someone else caught, cleaned, and cooked?

Make the choice to go out and seek your fortune and have authentic experiences. There is no substitute for taking your fate into your own hands and learning something important about the world and yourself, either through a thrilling victory or a crushing setback—or both. It truly is that simple.

Don't wait until you have the perfect plan or all the resources you need. Much of the value of adventuring is figuring out the plan as you go along and obtaining resources along the way through your wits and through the whims of good fortune and the kindness of strangers.

Live your life for a while as a series of journeys and jobs and projects that lead to adventures, resources, relationships, and fun. Don't be concerned about classmates who opt for more schooling or take a stepping-stone job they don't care about. There is no rush. You are not in a competition or in a race.

Have the adventures now that will no longer be possible once you have a spouse, children, a career, and a mortgage. Learn how the world works, and meet many different kinds of people. Get away from the distractions of your hometown and your family and your old friends. Fill your bag of experience so that later in life you don't have to rely on luck.

## Confronting Dragons

Jane Goodall felt the cold, wet shock of the chest-high grass against her bare skin. Her clothes were in a bundle above her head to keep them dry as she pushed through the sawtooth grass, dripping with chilly dew. Every morning, she dreaded leaving the warmth of her tent as she plunged alone into the dark Tanzanian dawn, making her way through an impenetrable forest along the way up to the Peak. She suffered scratches and cuts all over her body, but made the sacrifice for her groundbreaking work studying chimpanzees in the wild.

Goodall was very young and had no relevant education or training. She just knew she had to work with primates in Africa. And somehow, she had convinced world famous anthropologist Richard Leakey to take a chance on her. He wanted someone who wasn't biased by conventional scientific thinking on primate behavior. "My skin became hardened to the rough grasses of the valleys," wrote Goodall in her autobiography, *In the Shadow of Man* of the work progressing, "and my blood immune to the poison of the tsetse fly."

Life would be so easy if we could experience everything by watching it in a movie or looking at it in a controlled environment. But then those experiences would not truly belong to us. In order to have real adventures there have to be real risks, like those Goodall faced. Make certain you take the time to do something physical while you're young, whether it be challenging yourself in the outdoors or doing some kind of manual labor. Go explore the islands of Polynesia. Pan for gold in the Yukon. You have a full lifetime ahead for earning money with your mind, but now is the time to exchange sweat for knowledge and experience.

As a new adult, your objective should not be to seek a life of pampered luxury with all the risks removed and every comfort assured. Such a life would likely lead to boredom and depression. You weren't meant to win the lottery or live in paradise during the short window of new adulthood.

Your path requires you to relentlessly pursue dragons into the dark and overgrown forests where others are afraid to go and confront them.

Imagine a group of rock climbers at the base of a towering granite cliff preparing to make an ascent. Every bit of their skin that isn't covered by customized lightweight mountaineering gear is marked with the sunburns and cuts and scars of their passion for and commitment to climbing. It is evident from the way they check and double-check their gear that to climb this stone wall is to take on significant risk and to live close to the line. And those cuts and scars and mangled fingers are proof of the times they have crossed the line but returned for more.

To come away from the adventure stage of life with lessons and experiences will require you to live close to the line at times. Occasionally, you'll cross over. But it is better to take some calculated risk and end up with a few scars than to continually play it safe and forego the exhilaration of living on the edge. For an adventurer the goal isn't safety, it is to experience the unknown and learn valuable lessons in the process. And in order to have true adventures, you will need to invest your time and take some lumps. You want to climb mountains? Then you have to accept some sunburn on the back of your neck and some cuts on your hands. You want to study chimpanzees in the jungle? Then you have to accept brush abrasions and possibly malaria.

You don't need to risk your life in order for your adventures to be meaningful, but they aren't adventures if there isn't some risk inherent in them. Be smart. Do what you can to meticulously prepare, reduce the risk, and build in a margin of safety. Then, either move forward or, when necessary, say, "This is not beyond everyone's capabilities, but it is beyond mine, so I'm not going today." You'll be much happier having taken—or at least considered taking—some risk than you would by remaining on the sidelines.

## Traveling Light

During his hippie years in the 1970s, young Steve Jobs left Reed College in Oregon and traveled to India in search of enlightenment. He walked barefoot, slept in abandoned buildings, and a medicine man led him to the top of a mountain and shaved his head. India's poverty shocked Jobs deeply. He ran out of money and returned home from his adventures saying, "Thomas Edison [the inventor] did a lot more to improve the world than Karl Marx [the philosopher] and Neem Karoli Baba [an Indian guru] put together." A few years later, armed with this insight, he founded Apple.

The adventure stage of life is one of accumulating new experiences, self-knowledge, and relationships rather than one focused on attainment and pursuit of material riches. You are still young, and have the rest of your life for a career and earning money. For now, put your time and energy into exploration and meeting new people rather than into accumulating wealth. There will never be a better time to take some risks.

If you pursue an adventure and it turns out to have been a detour—like Job's search for an all-knowing guru in India—you have many years to recover. So travel as light as you can for now. Own a few items of clothing. Obtain a passport. Avoid accumulating bulky big-ticket items like furniture that can tie you to one location. Be able to pack a bag and leave immediately for the next opportunity.

There was a surfer in San Diego who received a Jeep from his father, a vintage car collector. It was a graduation gift, and his surf buddies seemed as excited about it as he did: "Come on, man, let's take a surf odyssey through Baja. We'll pay for the gas." But they received a surprising reply:

"Hey, guys, I would love to. But my dad gave me this Jeep to be the first car in my collection. I can't trash it in Mexico."

More than two of anything is a collection, and the last thing you want to do at this stage of life is to put your energy into being a collector. Collections and luxuries will force you into choices that pull you away from pursuing experience and learning and push you toward the burdens of maintaining and adding to your collection or indulging in the next luxury.

The beauty of life as a new adult is that you (hopefully) have good health and vitality and no long-term commitments. So use this window of time to full advantage. Rather than joining social clubs or frittering away your money on expensive clothes and meals, instead live simply and frugally and maximize your resources. Crash on friends' couches between adventures if you need to. Go on dates with fellow adventurers who are also traveling light and not seeking commitment. Don't let anything about your lifestyle compel you to say *no* when your college friends suggest traveling through India to pursue enlightenment or when your surf pals propose a Baja surf trip by Jeep.

In earning money to fund your adventures, let even your first jobs be adventures in and of themselves. As a teenager, Martha Stewart would take the bus from New Jersey to New York to work as photographer's model because it was fun and lucrative. "By trying out different businesses and jobs that interest you, you will learn things that will help you later," wrote the future billionaire lifestyle icon. "Experimentation is the only way to figure it out." You have to try a number of things to learn where your interests lie. Let work provide you with funds and serve as your teacher.

Have many adventures. And between adventures try different kinds of jobs. That will help you later when you are ready to fully enter the work world, as you will have a clearer idea of where your interests lie. You'll also identify a lot of jobs you never want to do again, like cleaning a dive bar at 3 a.m. after a night of debauchery or painting houses ten hours a day. Alternating between adventures and work will slowly begin revealing your true identity and teaching personal responsibility, hard work, camaraderie, and the importance of using your time to the fullest.

## Happiness vs. Fulfillment

"I've scored and assisted on lots of goals, won a bunch of honors," said Carli Lloyd, who at the time was a third-year All-American soccer player at Rutgers University, "and yet I still feel strangely unfulfilled." These amazingly prestigious accolades must have made Lloyd very happy and incredibly proud. But they did not lead to fulfillment for her.

A lot of confusion about the difference between happiness and fulfillment has been created in our modern society. Frequently movies and television will misuse the words "happiness" or "joy" when they are trying to convey that a character is seeking fulfillment.

Remember kindergarten birthdays? "It was the happiest day of my life. All my friends were sitting next to me and there were half-eaten pieces of pizza and empty juice boxes scattered around us. We were still soaking wet from an epic water-balloon fight. Then my parents brought out a humongous chocolate cake and everyone started singing 'Happy Birthday'..."

Imagine the *happiest* moment of your life. It probably involved some kind of celebration, games, fun, pleasure, enjoyment, and consumption. Now imagine the most *fulfilling* moment of a person's life. Fulfillment often comes at or near the end of sustained hard work, pain, exertion, sacrifice, and exhaustion. Think of a mother giving birth. Or a contractor completing years of work on a bridge or dam. Or a philanthropist leaving a fortune built over a lifetime to a cause or organization they care deeply about.

This is a book about how to pursue continuous fulfillment throughout one's life. It is a philosophy that views our lives as comprising five stages, each building upon the other. Fulfillment can be achieved through experiencing these life stages—adventures, mission, family, tribe, legacy—fully.

Everyone loves attending parties, having water-balloon fights, and eating pizza and cake, but there is nothing uniquely personal or meaningful underlying those activities.

Fulfillment cannot be obtained by doing something solely in order to be wealthy. Or to be famous. Or to make parents proud. Or to keep one's options open. Or to make one's insecurities go away. Fulfillment cannot be achieved by going to the best parties, or by living in the best house, or by wearing the best clothes. Nor will sustained happiness be achieved through the enjoyment of hobbies, food, drink, sex, or illicit substances. No person has ever partied or consumed their way into a fulfilling life.

Steady progress through life's stages and performing each stage to the best of our abilities—with a unique *mission* as the centerpiece—is the path to sustained fulfillment and enduring personal success. What makes living a life of continuous fulfillment both so challenging and so rewarding is that the life stages are not always sequential. There will be times of overlap, which will require thoughtful choices. Fulfillment is the absence of depression, and depression is the absence of fulfillment. Fulfillment will ultimately be accomplished by figuring out what we were born to do and spending our lives doing it.

Lloyd worked with Australian trainer James Galanis to convert her experiences and adventures as a college and Junior National Team soccer player into a mission. They created a detailed mission plan for Lloyd to become the best soccer player in the world. She worked harder than ever before. And she experienced fulfillment through accomplishing her mission as she led her teams to Olympic gold and World Cup victories.

Pursuing wealth, fame, or power as ends in and of themselves or to impress others, is a false objective. Living life on your own terms in the pursuit of fulfillment is the true objective. And in this pursuit *your adventures are your foundation*. Because as was the case for Goodall, Jobs, and Lloyd, your adventures will inform your mission. Fulfillment will ensue from performing the life stages well. And that begins with challenging yourself now through a series of adventures and figuring out who *you* are.

## Cobble Together Successes

"I was trained for absolutely nothing...but I had the gift of gab...and could either talk my way in our out of a situation, or if necessary, fight my way in or out." Within a few years Australian actor Errol Flynn would be regarded as the "most magnetic, most charming man in the world." He would begin a meteoric ascent culminating in becoming Hollywood's biggest movie star. But at the time he said this, he was 20 years old, done with school, and adventuring in untamed New Guinea.

There was a gold rush in progress in New Guinea in 1929 and Flynn dreamed of striking it rich. He cobbled together a small grubstake by working as a charter captain and took Hollywood producer, Joel Swartz, up the crocodile- and cannibal-infested Sepik River. Swartz filmed a documentary (through which Flynn was later "discovered"). Flynn used the funds he earned to march inland for a week with a crew of kanakas and staked a gold claim at Edey Creek. When he and his men were attacked by headhunters, he had to return to civilization. But another group of prospectors tracked him down and bought his claim because it abutted their own. Flynn used the money to purchase the decrepit sailing ship *Sirocco*. He sailed thirty miles north of Port Moresby and unexpectedly fell in love with the emerald green countryside around the Laloki River. On the spot, he decided to sell the *Sirocco*, and used the proceeds to establish a tobacco plantation at Laloki.

That's a fanciful and no doubt embellished version of how it works, but in practice the basic concept still holds. You don't go from hired charter captain to tobacco plantation owner all in one move. You cobble together small successes into larger and larger ones. You parlay A into B, and B into C, and keep going until you reach the final objective.

Don't allow your adventure-fueled progress to be stalled. Everything in this world is always either expanding or contracting. So it is up to you to keep parlaying your current hand into an even bigger and better one. After your initial set of adventures begins to inform you about yourself and where your desires and aspirations lay, it is time to start carefully planning your next set of adventures and ensure you are not leaving your lifepath to chance. Formulate the specific goals you hope to achieve through your upcoming adventures. Replace dreams with objectives.

Set aside time each day to think about your goals and write them down. Introspection requires time free from distraction, and it is difficult to distill your goals without it. Make a to-do list every evening for the next day. It can't be understated how important it is to have a written plan for each day. Unpack your brain by putting your thoughts on paper, and then take the time you need to review and improve them. Be organized and make plans, but don't let your lists and organization systems become ends unto themselves. To-do lists and plans are meant to be ripped up and replaced with improved ones as your adventures progress and your goals evolve.

As you move deeper into the adventure stage, it is time to start to understand the difference between creating and receiving. Through your adventures you *receive* enjoyment, resources, and knowledge about yourself. Use this information to *create* new plans for more adventures, which will generate more enjoyment, resources, and knowledge. It is up to you to create a framework for your life. Through your adventures you will receive what you need to fill in the framework.

This distinction came into play for Errol Flynn as well. He built a large comfortable house of palm and bamboo, a tobacco barn, and a curing furnace. His crop thrived in the New Guinean heat and humidity. "I stared at the tobacco field, all my fortune in it," he wrote in his autobiography, *My Wicked, Wicked Ways*. "The leaves were green. The sun was warming the crop. I could smell the tobacco leaf." The reasons for Flynn's later success as a Hollywood swashbuckler are clear. He had truly lived the life of an adventurer and leader before making films, and audiences were mesmerized by the authenticity of his performances.

**From Innocence to Experience**

"I was a depressed teenager," said guitarist Jane Wiedlin, a young adult in 1980s Los Angeles. "I thought life was completely pointless when I was in high school, but just a few short years later, I was having the adventure of a lifetime in a successful rock band."

Classes and books can teach you facts and theories and techniques, but they can't give you experience or help you discover who you are. Since you entered high school you've worked hard and learned from your teachers and textbooks. But now you that you've graduated, you need to go beyond your coursework and learn from direct experience. It is time to have adventures and seek your fortune.

"Looking back, my life at that time stands out as surreal, colorful, vibrant…. I didn't have any money but felt like I owned the town," said another young adult, Belinda Carlisle, who was immersing herself in the Sunset Strip's live music scene in Hollywood. "Occasionally, I was onstage as a backup singer, other times I was in the audience, but I was living the dream all the time."

Whether you are a musician, surfer, primatologist, soccer player, pilot, tobacco farmer, or an actor—or if you pursue any other path—you won't end up having anything original and valuable to contribute to the world if you remain at home in a comfortable room with people and knowledge from your school days. Reading a book about wine won't teach you like trying wine for yourself. You must seek out adventures and experiences that will force you to think for yourself and throw you into extreme situations populated by eccentric characters who can show you how the world works.

Wiedlin immersed herself in the Los Angeles punk music scene. She also worked at a fashion design house, and she would scribble lyrics on the clothing patterns scattered around her. Carlisle rented an apartment in Hollywood so she could attend as many live shows as possible on the strip: "The parties that followed the shows were as important to us insiders as the shows themselves. They gave everyone a chance to mingle, talk about the performances, compare what we'd seen and heard." Based on these conversations, Carlisle made a trip to London, as many of the acts performing in Hollywood had come from there.

During your student days, your teachers prepared you and your classmates with the same material for the same exams. That approach won't work now. You each have a different path. Your obligation to yourself is to have experiences and learn lessons that will reveal your own unique path. Seek out people who are like what you want to be. Once you embark on your journey you will find that the universe is a fantastic educator. Let the world create the circumstances you need to meet like-minded people and absorb new knowledge. With each new experience your path will become clearer.

At a party Carlisle spoke with Wiedlin and bassist Margot Olaverra about the bands they'd seen in Hollywood, San Francisco, and London. "Eventually we were talking about starting our own band," said Carlisle. They added drummer Elissa Bello and guitarist Charlotte Caffey. "We hadn't even played a gig but we were already talking as if there was nothing more real and happening than our band," said Carlisle. From the start the "five personalities immediately added up to something that was greater than any of us as individuals could have ever been. It was the right chemistry."

The band decided to call themselves the Go-Go's, because it meant "uninhibited and free." Their first single, *We Got the Beat*, was a hit. They performed for a year and then made a record. A raw, adventurous spirit had brought them together—and their fans felt and responded to it. The Go-Go's were the first (and are still the only) all-female rock band who played their own instruments and wrote their own songs to create a number-one album: *Beauty and the Beat*.

## Run Your Own Race

"I knew that dogfighting was what I was born to do," wrote Chuck Yeager, a World War II fighter pilot. "Concentration was total; you remained focused, ignoring fatigue or fear.... Once you zeroed in, began to outmaneuver your opponent while closing in, you became a cat with a mouse, and there was no way out: You both knew he was finished." Yeager was a teenager when he joined the Air Force and became an ace in his early 20s.

After his adventures as a fighter pilot, Yeager chose to remain in the military and work as a test pilot. In the remote Mojave Desert, he became the first person to break the sound barrier. He said, "I wasn't a deep, sophisticated person, but I lived by a basic principle: I did only what I enjoyed. I wouldn't let anyone derail me by promises of power or money into doing things that weren't interesting...job titles didn't mean diddly."

If you've ever had a friend or a cousin or a neighbor who is really passionate about something—be it archery, horseback riding, or brewing their own beer—and have seen them with a group of their friends who are into the same thing, there's a lot you can learn. There's a certain way they talk with one another, often using words you've never heard. A way they dress and adorn themselves when they are about to go for a ride. An attitude they exude as they gear up to compete. There's a whole lifestyle and way of doing things that goes with their passion. And to the outsider it may seem very strange and weird, but to them it makes complete sense and seems perfectly normal—and they wouldn't change it for anything.

Most new adults are surrounded by peers who are confused, because they don't know who they are yet and are trying to please or impress the people around them. Don't fall into that trap. Just be who you are rather than turning yourself into a composite of what you think other people want you to be. Go ahead and be as strange and weird and authentic and true to yourself as you wish.

During the adventure stage of life let the outer layers of your personality that were perhaps put there by others start to slip away. Determine who you are underneath. Don't worry about occupational or material accolades for now. Just make steady progress along your adventure path and be the best and most genuine version of yourself. Remain true to yourself and do things at your own pace and on your own timetable.

Have you ever watched the Daytona 500? It is difficult to know after the first lap who is going to win because there are still 199 laps left to go. Maybe the driver who is leading after the first lap went out too fast and is going to overheat or end up not having enough fuel many laps from now. Maybe a driver who is in the middle of the pack now had the better plan and will execute better and ultimately win it all. You have to run your own race your own way. You should never assume the other driver is ahead. It may not even be a race at all. Maybe you can accomplish what you were meant to accomplish and so will the other person, and it only looks at the present moment like you are competing with each other.

Even after he became internationally famous for breaking the sound barrier, Yeager said of his comrades: "It was a tight little circle. My life was flying and pilots. At a party we were like a bunch of doctors, talking a lingo no outsider could understand…. Being famous with the public meant absolutely nothing to a guy living out in the middle of the Mojave Desert."

Engineer your life to suit your core essence, talents, and tastes. Develop friends and mentors who can help you make progress. Live in a place and in a manner that is conducive to immersing yourself further in your passion. The truth is everyone loves having an eccentric, unconventional friend who dresses and acts strangely and brings positive energy and enthusiasm and color with them wherever they go. And everyone secretly wishes they had the courage to truly be themselves too.

## We're in This Together

Joanne and her chums began a drunken rendition of "You Make Me Feel Like a Natural Woman," by Aretha Franklin. They had piled into Katrina McKinnon's car for a road trip and were on their way back to campus from the Black Horse pub for a dorm room chat. Joanne, later known as J. K. Rowling, the billionaire author of the *Harry Potter* books, "always enjoyed the company of her female friends, an informal gang or sisterhood who discussed each other's problems, which were usually the men in their lives," said Rowling's former Exeter University classmate, Yvette Cowles.

As far as adventures go, road trips are hard to beat. The open road, sun overhead, windows open, music blasting, on your way to yet another town you've never visited before. Needless to say, a good friend is in the seat next to you and you're already embellishing and laughing about the various incidents that happened in the town you just left. No timetable, and nowhere you need to be. What could be better than that?

When you're in cahoots with a comrade, it's pure joy. You are at ease but totally in the moment. Ready for anything and everything. You know you're going to have some fun, whether the next town welcomes you with open arms and new experiences or even if your car breaks down before you get there. The theme is always, "We're in this together." Sometimes with optimism and anticipation of what lies around the next turn. Sometimes with a little shared grumbling as you help each other extricate yourselves from a problem or predicament that one of you caused.

The reason these relationships are so satisfying, easy, and fun is that you are peers. Equals. You'll never be at ease like this with someone who is ten years older than you, or ten years younger than you, or with someone you work for, or who works for you. Making fun of your comrade or teasing them in a good-natured way every once in a while—about their trendy new haircut or that ugly shirt they just overpaid for—helps season the relationship and allows you to keep each other on track. People on different levels of some hierarchy don't get to do that.

Show respect for your friends by assuming they can overcome the challenges in their own lives rather than offering unsolicited advice. Pay your comrades the ultimate compliment by asking for their help or advice in your life when you need it. Be a person who always answers the question, "Will you help me?" with, "Definitely! What do you need?"

Some comrades are with us for just a short time of mutual benefit—classmates, teammates, coworkers. Don't put too much pressure on these relationships or have unreasonable expectations. Other friends will be with us for life and will overlap with us many times—as neighbors, bridal-party members, and coaches for our kids' teams. Shared history across multiple roles as friends is truly priceless. Keep in mind that you never want to be in an uneven friendship. Relationships always seem to work best when each person has something that can help the other and when each has a talent or capability that the other does not.

To develop true friendship and get past talking about sports and the weather, you have to let yourself be vulnerable. You have to reveal who you are below the surface, little by little, over time. And that requires choosing friends who reciprocate your trust and keep what you reveal in confidence.

"The time has come for me to write a full confession of my life to you," wrote Jack Kerouac in 1950 in response to a 12,000-word letter from his friend Neal Cassady. At the time he was working on what would later become his groundbreaking novel, *On the Road*, chronicling his cross country driving adventures with Cassady. Kerouac practically invented the concept of the road trip, and the *we're in this together* ethos was a major reason *On the Road* has been so popular for decades. He famously advised us all to "live, travel, adventure, bless, and don't be sorry."

## Seize Opportunity

"It is a cross between a flophouse and a gold mine," said Conrad Hilton, excitedly describing the Mobley Hotel to a prospective investor. Hilton, who would eventually establish the international Hilton Hotels conglomerate, also said candidly, "Just be glad the people around town have so much oil in their eyes they can't see it."

After growing up in New Mexico, Hilton originally planned to become a banker. As a young adult in the 1920s, he traveled to Texas to seek his fortune during the oil boom. With $5,000 he had borrowed he negotiated the purchase of a bank. But seeing Hilton's eagerness the owner of the bank increased the price after the purchase terms had been agreed upon. Hilton decided to walk away because he saw an even better opportunity. He decided to purchase the hotel he had been lodging in, the Mobley Hotel. There was so much demand that the owner had to resort to turning the hotel guests out of their rooms every eight hours. It became the first hotel in a global empire Hilton assembled.

Windows of opportunity are very small. You have to be able to recognize them and be ready and willing to step through them without hesitation. During the Apollo lunar mission era, rockets could only be launched at certain times of day when lighting and temperature were optimal, when atmospheric pressure conditions including absence of clouds were optimal, and when the position of Earth relative to the moon was optimal. NASA engineers and mission planners had to work backward from projected windows of good conditions and make highly detailed plans in order to have the lunar rocket, the launch tower, the astronauts, and thousands of mission personnel all ready to go at the same time.

Imagine if an Apollo mission had been forced to launch a day late because one of the astronauts had written down the wrong launch date. Or, what if rather than targeting a specific date based on forecast conditions the mission team simply picked their favorite day of the week because "Wednesday is our lucky day." The results could have been catastrophic. You have to seize opportunities when the external conditions are right rather than when you happen to be ready. And you must never rely on luck alone.

You most likely will not have a massive team of the world's greatest minds working with unlimited resources on determining the ideal window of opportunity for your endeavors like the Apollo astronauts did. So you have to learn how to recognize great opportunities for yourself. Don't expect to easily find them. Most of the low-lying fruit tends to be picked off by veterans and insiders. And you can't wait passively for good luck to hand you anything in life, because such gifts are often susceptible to being lost through bad luck.

Mark Zuckerberg has been rightfully criticized for his tongue-in-cheek motto, "Move fast and break things." People also jokingly say, "It is better to beg forgiveness than ask permission." But a useful kernel lies within both of these sayings. As long as you are not knowingly harming others, be guided by seizing opportunity rather than by fearing problems or fallout.

When a team wins a championship, you will sometimes hear critics say they only won because of injuries to opponents, an easy schedule, favorable weather, or some other external factor. But using such factors to gain an edge is the definition of seizing opportunity, and is the norm rather than the exception in overcoming attrition and winning the final game.

Having lost the opportunity to purchase the bank, Hilton wasn't going to miss out again. He seized the Mobley Hotel opportunity without delay. Within twenty-four hours of approaching the hotel's owner he had sent telegrams to investors and raised the funds he needed. As Hilton wrote in his autobiography, *Be My Guest*, "The following day, at noon, the Mobley changed hands. I was in the hotel business." That night Hilton slept in the Mobley's office, because all the guest rooms were rented. He slept soundly and "dreamed of Texas wearing a chain of Hilton hotels."

## Mentors "Pass Through"

"As his apprentice—I started when I was about three—I was charged with removing weeds...with a flathead screwdriver," said legendary lifestyle entrepreneur Martha Stewart. As her first mentor, Martha's father instilled in his daughter a love of gardening. She later cultivated additional mentors such as Julia Child, Rupert Murdoch, and Warren Buffett.

Sometimes a young person is fortunate enough to have a wise and caring elder pass through their life for a period of time and change their trajectory forever. Phil Jackson passed through Michael Jordan's life during a nine-year period and assisted him in becoming the best and most successful basketball player of his generation.

Jackson was 17 years older than Jordan. His playing days were behind him and he was coaching in Canada in the 1980s while Jordan was a young player lighting up the NBA for the Chicago Bulls. But though he received many individual honors, Jordan was unable to break through and lead his team to an NBA championship. Then Jackson was recruited to coach the Bulls. During their time together they led the Bulls to one of the greatest championship runs in professional sports history with six NBA titles in eight seasons.

Those facts are well known. But what doesn't get as much attention is that Jackson was much more than a coach to Jordan. He was a mentor. He had won an NBA championship as a player and a CBA championship as a coach, but he had also been raised by two ministers and spirituality was a primary component of his life. Sure, he had basketball knowledge (as all basketball coaches do) and championship knowledge (as a few basketball

YOUR LIFEPATH | 19

coaches do) but he also brought interpersonal knowledge and spirituality knowledge to Jordan.

A mentor is an older and more experienced person who offers wisdom, counsel and support to a younger person. Usually, the age gap between mentor and protégé is about eight to 25 years. You'll receive *advice* on many topics throughout your life, but what makes mentorship distinct is that it is sustained guidance in an area which connects to your life mission.

As you pursue your adventures and go deeper into areas you are most interested in—be it basketball, gardening, investing, or writing a cookbook—you will run into older and more experienced people, some of whom could be your mentors. Look for someone who has done what you hope to do. Jackson, for example, had played on an NBA championship team, whereas Jordan's previous Bulls coach, Doug Collins, had not.

Keep in mind, though, that an older person who achieved their success either through sheer raw talent or through family connections may not have as much to teach you as a person who worked their way up from the bottom over a long period of time. Make certain to find mentors who can help you discover and pursue your own unique path rather pushing you to do things exactly as they did on their path. Adapt a mentor's wisdom and methods to the specifics of your situation.

Michael Jordan and Phil Jackson produced amazing results together, but ultimately they each moved on from the Bulls. As is typically the case with mentor-protégé relationships, circumstances bring them together and later circumstances move them toward other relationships. Jordan later became part owner of the NBA's Charlotte Bobcats and Jackson coached and mentored other players to five more NBA championships with the Los Angeles Lakers.

Martha Stewart long ago went from being a protégé to becoming a mentor herself. She famously took rapper Snoop Dogg, under her wing in 2008 after they met when he was a guest on her cooking show. During that initial appearance he was all thumbs and could barely peel a potato, but he has now become a lifestyle icon in his own right—and an excellent cook.

## A Collection of Winning Pieces

In 1915, disaster struck when Ernest Shackleton's ship, the *Endurance*, became frozen in the Antarctic ice. It was the height of what has now become known as the Heroic Age of Antarctic Exploration, and Shackleton was trying to make history by leading the first trans-Antarctic expedition. After six months of the *Endurance* being slowly crushed by the incredible weight of the ice, Shackleton and his crew had to abandon it as it started to sink. They were left adrift, living in tents on open ice sheets for months, and eventually made their way to Elephant Island off the southern tip of Africa.

The greatest adventures of all time and the greatest stories ever told are about explorers and buccaneers having to overcome challenges with scant resources. Shackleton and his crew—living off snow melt and penguin blubber while maximizing every resource they could muster to survive for many months and return to safety a year after the *Endurance* first became locked in ice—is a prime example.

Adventures, almost by definition, involve a leap of faith into the unknown with resources that may be insufficient to take you as far as you need to go. Like an explorer preparing for an expedition, put together a collection of winning pieces for yourself by examining your life and inventorying everything in it. *Learn to use your resourcefulness to overcome your lack of resources.*

Allocate more effort and energy into those areas that bring you enjoyment and where you are generating successes. Allow those areas that feel tedious or like a nuisance to slowly fade away. Create a streamlined collection of complementary resources, platforms, and relationships. Collect those things that taken together help you grow stronger, more capable, and better positioned every day for the next success.

Like Errol Flynn in New Guinea, learn how to politick or fight your way into any opportunity or out of any problem. With that skill set you will always be in a position to accumulate more of what works and eliminate more of what doesn't. Cultivate a relaxed but determined demeanor. Be alert during your adventures, like a wolf in the forest, and live in the absolute present. Stay vigilant to *perceive* patterns, synchronicities and transfers of energy in the world around you. Ask yourself, *Why is this happening? What does this mean?* Then take action based upon your conclusions.

Adventures, and the lessons we are meant to learn from them, unfold in their own time. That doesn't mean a straight line that either moves fast or moves slow. It means smaller or larger zigzags. Or even shipwrecks like Shackleton experienced. And it is within these zigs and zags that we have epiphanies and learn lessons. That is where the most interesting parts of our lives take place. That is where we learn how to maximize our resources.

Avoid outgoing annuities of time, energy, and dollars. Fulfill yourself emotionally and materially through the pursuit of your adventures and through your relationships. During the adventure stage—and beyond—avoid trying to fulfill yourself through illicit activities, consumption, or possessions. Preserve time for fun, thinking, and to gain insight and enlightenment. Do what is enjoyable, serves a purpose, and adds to your collection of winning pieces.

Above all, learn how to ride a good situation as long and as far as you can. Most expeditions, ventures, relationships, jobs, teams, and projects will ultimately end. They aren't meant to last forever. Think of them as ships—like the *Endurance*—that are supposed to take you part of the way on a very long journey. When one leg of the journey ends, don't be upset or surprised. Be grateful to the ship you were on for the miles you were able to travel and for the progress you were able to make, and find a way to keep going. As Shackleton said, "I believe it is in our nature to explore, to reach out into the unknown. The only true failure would be not to explore at all."

## You *Are* Your Behavior

"At age sixteen I decided to quit high school, pack my bags, and move to England to pursue racing," wrote Danica Patrick in her autobiography, *Danica–Crossing the Line*. She had won three World Karting Association national championships, and now wanted to transition from go-karts to racecars. She chose to hone her craft racing Formula One cars on the European circuit.

In England, with no parents setting boundaries for her, Patrick began drinking more to fit in with the other racers. "We all drank way more than we should have. Going to the pub after practice to have a few beers or cocktails was part of our English existence." Her sponsor heard about Patrick's hard partying, and at the end of the season terminated her sponsorship, because she wasn't fully dedicated to racing. It appeared to be the end of her dreams of one day becoming a professional racer.

During the adventure stage of life, it is your job to accumulate experience, knowledge, and the self-awareness that will allow you to succeed and live a fulfilling life. One of the most valuable lessons you must learn, and which many others build outwards from, is to come to the understanding that *you are your behavior*.

You are not how you *intended* to behave or *wish* you had behaved or how you behave when others are observing you. Those who want to will always find a way to meet their obligations. And those who don't will always find an excuse. Every person deserves the way they are perceived by others, be it positive or negative. If another person has a poor impression of you, don't bother saying, "That's not me!" It *is* you—your cumulative behavior.

At first Patrick lied to her parents and made excuses to explain her drinking and carousing. But eventually she accepted responsibility and asked her sponsor for another chance. She was allowed to race another season in England, but had to agree to live with a family under their supervision.

As you go beyond what you learned from your parents and at school, you can develop a deeper understanding of values and character. Begin that process by truly examining your behavior:

- *Do you always tell the truth?* Lies are monsters that run wild and demolish everything they touch. Lies are exhausting to everyone. Always tell the truth and willingly accept the consequences.
- *Do you make excuses for shortcomings that are within your control?* Your explanations don't excuse you from meeting your obligations.
- *Do you let your accomplishments speak for themselves?* If you've done anything worthwhile, you don't need to brag. The world knows.
- *Are you friendly, polite, enthusiastic, and great to be around?* Every company, team, tribe and community will want you if you are.
- *Do you ever act inferior or superior to anyone?* If you do, try to determine why you have two different sets of behaviors.

"It definitely solidified my notion of right and wrong," said Patrick of her first year in England. "You don't miss anything new by missing a party. They're always the same. People drink, they dance, they get stupid, and then they puke or pass out." She improved greatly the next two years. Eventually she won the 2008 Indy Japan 300, the only win by a woman in an Indy Car Series race.

Ultimately, our lives are nothing more than a collection of our choices meant to accomplish our objectives. Now that you are out in the world, adventuring and pursuing your lifepath, you have to make choices every day about what your behavior is going to be and who you *are*.

## Refining Your Personal Code

"I'll fight you on one foot! I'll fight you with my eyes closed!" bellowed the Lion, shadowboxing like a prizefighter and throwing air punches. Dorothy, the Scarecrow, and the Tin Man scattered to get away from this pompous blowhard who had blocked their path on the Yellow Brick Road. Then the Lion lunged at Dorothy's pet dog, Toto. Without thinking she jumped forward and slapped him, "Shame on you! Why don't you pick on something bigger than you?" From that point onward in the *The Wizard of Oz*, everyone's character begins to grow and grow and grow.

Adventures reveal character. Character is a personal commitment to do what is right at all times, even if to do so comes at great personal cost. A person of good character makes choices and takes action based on internalized constant principles. To have good character is to be honest, reliable, self-disciplined, helpful to others, and above all accountable for the consequences of one's choices and decisions.

The adventurers we admire from ancient history, literature, and myth chose to live their lives according to a deeply held code of conduct and character. This code of character embodies a very high set of ideals that a hero feels compelled to live up to. And the stories about these heroes that we enjoy so much are those surrounding the challenges and difficulties they have to face in adhering to their code in extreme circumstances.

The Knights of the Round Table followed the code of chivalry. The Japanese samurai were bound by the code of *bushido*. Wonder Woman adheres to the utopian philosophies of the Amazons. James Bond is an English gentleman. Obi Wan Kenobi and Ahsoka Tano follow the Jedi code.

On the other hand, for a person with poor character anything is justifiable, and for any mistake a rationalization can be used to put the blame on someone else. Such a person has no internal core set of values, and so is constantly changing their behavior as new whims occur to them, or deciding what results they want first and then working their standards backward. A person with poor character makes choices based on raw impulses, appetites, urges, and desires.

A personal code of character comprises five main principles:

- *Do the right thing at all times.* Don't lie, cheat, or steal. Avoid hurting other people whenever possible. Follow the rules.

- *Meet your obligations.* Do what you say you're going to do. Follow through and be dependable. Be loyal to your friends, family, co-workers, teammates, etc.

- *Be self-disciplined.* Don't act in haste. Think about the consequences your actions will have on other people. Be productive.

- *Own your decisions.* Stand by what you've done without blaming others or circumstances. Make amends if you harm someone.

- *Help those who can't help themselves.* Offer assistance to the young, the old, the sick, and those who are down on their luck.

Dorothy recruited the Cowardly Lion to join her friends on their path to the Emerald City. And by the end of the *Wizard of Oz*, the Lion has shown he is actually very brave and loyal. He carries his friends on his back, and he helps Dorothy complete her journey.

Develop and refine your personal code of character through your adventures, for it is essential to your successes in the future life stages. Follow Dorothy's example. Stand up for those who can't defend themselves, and befriend comrades who are dependable. Seek to join forces with fellow travelers of good character with whom you can share your journey and whose motivations and behaviors you can understand and predict.

**Be Great, not Perfect**

Nadia Comaneci, a 14-year-old Romanian gymnast, gathered momentum at the end of her routine and exploded off the uneven bars high in the air and stuck her landing. As she took her bow, the fans all around her erupted with applause and the unthinkable happened. One after another, the judges awarded her a perfect score of 10 for her routine. Not only had no athlete ever scored a perfect 10 in an Olympic event before, but the scoreboard at the 1976 Montreal Olympics wasn't even able to display a *10* and had to show her score as *1.00*. For a few brief seconds Comaneci was flawless. And that is just about the best any human being can do.

The world isn't perfect. And neither is anything or any person in it. Continuous and sustained flawlessness is impossible. So we must channel our energy into striving for excellence and into becoming great rather than into chasing perfection.

The enduring myths of the ancient past feature heroes like Achilles, who was more or less invulnerable and perfect other than his secret weakness, his 'Achilles heel'. The 20th century gave us Superman, who can't be hurt or defeated other than by his one weakness, kryptonite. Without these imperfections, neither Achilles nor Superman would be able to do anything heroic, because they would be gods.

Perfectionism is often associated with disillusionment, because the world and everything and everyone in it have flaws and imperfections. It is an impossible task to cobble imperfect ingredients into a perfect result. However, rather than seeking to eliminate all weaknesses and flaws in yourself, you can seek to maximize results by focusing on building up your strengths. Nobody has ever succeeded by having no flaws, but everyone who does succeed has to find a way to work around and compensate for those flaws. The way to do that is by figuring out where your own personal strengths are and creating your own personalized style and strategies for accentuating your strengths and minimizing your weaknesses.

On the other hand, just because you weren't born perfect doesn't mean you should use that as an excuse not to aim high in life. You weren't born perfect, and nobody else was either. Every person ever born could blame their shortcomings on bad parents, or being too tall or too short, or their blotchy skin, or their lack of math skills, or being born on the wrong continent in the wrong century. None of those shortcomings is your fault, but that doesn't relieve you of the obligation to do the best you can with the positive attributes and abilities you were blessed with at birth.

Reading the biographies of the greats throughout history will reveal that nobody has had a perfect run. Everyone has been born with imperfections and challenges to overcome. Muhammad was an orphan. Moses was born to parents who were slaves. Confucius lost his father while he was very young. Learn from how hard they worked, and always know that you have the capability to do even greater things than they ever did. Always remind yourself that you are equal to the best and can go beyond.

The kings and generals and philosophers of ancient times whose marks upon the world have proved to be indelible never aspired primarily be rich or famous or perfect. They aspired to be *great*. The ultimate accolade was to be called Alexander the Great, not Perfect King Alexander or Alexander the Rich & Famous. Fame and riches, if they are to mean anything, are a by-product of living by an internal code of character, striving for excellence and accomplishing great deeds.

These days, 10s for gymnastic routines are more common. But to this day there is no athlete who has had a perfect run through an entire Olympics or through life. The ongoing inclination to strive toward being as flawless and great as possible is more important than a perfect score in and of itself.

## Make Others Feel Good

"What the fuck are you doing?!... What don't you fucking understand?!... Fuck's sake, you're an amateur!" On the set of *Terminator Salvation*, lead actor Christian Bale unleashed a four-minute rant on the lighting director, accusing him of "trashing my scene."

Bale apologized to all afterward, and also issued several public apologies after an unauthorized recording of the tirade made its way to the internet. He asked people not to allow his "incredibly embarrassing meltdown to overshadow this movie." Other actors came forward to defend Bale and explained that he was playing a post-apocalyptic messiah fighting to save the world from evil cyborgs, and had become temporarily confused by method acting and having immersed himself so completely in a role.

They say that an actor has to make certain not to fall into the *existential fallacy* of treating a character they play as real. The Terminator isn't real. And John Connor, the savior being played by Christian Bale, isn't real. They are both illusions that were brought to life onstage during filming.

The key to winning the goodwill of your fellow adventurers and others in your life is good manners. Not just in the traditional sense of always saying *please* and *thank you*. But rather by coming to a deeper understanding of the *self*. The self is an external projection and an illusion, separate from a person's internal core essence. Often the self is like a role in a movie. Much of a person's decision-making each day arises not from reason or logic, but from emotions arising from a very deep need to build and protect this illusory self or role. What we think of as good manners are often nothing more than treating another person's illusion or projection of self with care and understanding.

Recognize that often the people we interact with become confused by bravado or other behaviors of the self-image they are projecting, which is different from who they are on the inside. Having good manners means you make other people feel cared for, respected, and understood. Always go out of your way to make other people feel good:

- *Give undivided attention.* Recognize that focused time and sustained attention are the greatest gifts we can give or receive. Have an elegant, graceful, unrushed manner in all your interactions.

- *Develop rapport with others.* True rapport is developed by genuinely making other people feel good with no ulterior motive. Alternate between listening to what matters to them and making them smile with an interesting comment or quip.

- *Avoid self-importance.* Steer clear of conspicuous consumption and attention-seeking behavior. Never correct people or throw your weight around. Don't put others on a pedestal either.

- *Discuss but don't attack.* Enjoy spirited discussion and occasional disagreement with your companions. Debate a position but never attack a person. Simply say, "That's an interesting perspective."

- *Encourage rather than criticize.* Seek to help people who are sad or depressed by encouraging them. Fill people up with the warmth of your affirmative energy and with subtle but sincere compliments.

Be a person your fellow adventurers and other people in your life gravitate toward. Make them feel comfortable in seeking you out, because they know you always make them feel respected and secure. A basic tenet of winning friends is to be a good listener, which is great advice. But be a good talker too. Everyone loves a positive, interesting, and on-point talker who is succinct and knows how to bring out commonalities.

Above all, when anyone engages you in conversation, listen to their words—but make certain to dig below the surface. Try to determine, "What does this person *need* from me?"

## Volcanic Moments

"The body of the elephant was swaying," wrote Beryl Markham, who was raised in Africa and was one of the only female safari pilots during the golden age of flying. "It was like watching a boulder, in whose path you were trapped, teeter on the edge of a cliff before plunging."

Markham had recently left her family's farm in Kenya to pursue adventures as a pilot. She was assisting her safari clients in the bush when an enormous elephant broke off from the herd to confront them. From just ten feet away, "he began the elephant scream of anger, which is so terrifying as to hold you silent where you stand, like fingers clamped upon your throat."

We've all seen people scream, bark, or growl, without apparent provocation. Maybe we have done so ourselves. Most angry people don't know what they are really angry about. Often an angry person is not truly angry about what is happening now. They're often angry about a number of things that led to this volcanic moment.

During the adventure stage you will put yourself in some extreme and unfamiliar situations. This is the best time in your life to learn how to keep your emotions and your self-control in check. As a starting point, always assume that the world is trying to provide for you rather than out to get you. Have empathy for everyone you interact with. Rarely is anyone actively trying to be your adversary. Seek to understand the other person's motivations and to bend interactions to mutual benefit. And when you react to events, always try your best to be a lady or gentleman.

Be strong. On occasion everyone goes through times of being annoyed or disappointed, but keep things in perspective. Differentiate between the root cause and the symptom. Don't lose your temper over problems that have solutions. Instead, put your energy into solving them. And don't lose your temper over problems that have no solutions, because that is simply a waste of your time. Never do, say, or write anything you can't walk back. Ask yourself: *A week from now will I be glad I blew up over this, or will I wish I'd waited a day?*

Be strategic. The only times you should ever display true anger, lash out verbally, or consider using force are when you, your family, or your comrades are being physically threatened, and all other avenues for resolving a situation have failed. Don't confront anyone without having first exhausted all other options. Don't confront anyone without having your temper in check. Don't confront anyone without being willing to live with the consequences for the rest of your life.

Life isn't like a movie where there has to be a shouting match or a fistfight every time a character is annoyed by something or blocked by an obstacle. It is ultimately a lot more satisfying to overcome obstacles and get the upper hand on annoyances in our own way and on our own timetable rather than through a dramatic on-the-spot showdown. The aftereffect of an angry episode can linger like a hangover, so do your best to avoid them.

The hunters knew their guns were useless. "Bullets would sink into that monstrous hide like pebbles into a pond," wrote Markham. But fortunately, the elephant screamed again, which frightened the herd and forced the elephant to have to turn and rejoin it. The elephant's own anger and lack of self-control had saved Markham and her clients. She lived on to become a record-setting aviatrix and an internationally acclaimed author of the book *West with the Night*, chronicling her adventures flying in Africa and setting aviation records.

In our youth we may believe arguing or fighting is often the best solution to a problem. But many times the impulse to spar is really just an attempt at avoiding the work that goes with persuading. As we grow older we eventually come to realize there are only a handful of times in our lives when there aren't much better solutions.

## Training and Observation

Miyamoto Musashi left home at sixteen to embark on a "warrior pilgrimage" in the year 1600 and went on to become Japan's greatest samurai, defeating more than sixty opponents in sword duels. Ted Williams began playing minor league baseball in 1936 at seventeen years old and went on to become the greatest hitter who ever lived, a nineteen-time all-star and the last MLB player to hit over .400 for a full season. Though separated by three centuries and an ocean, the two men had much in common.

In addition to his acclaim as a swordsman, Musashi also went to war to fight with the Ashikaga army against Shogun Ieyasu, and survived a massacre in which 70,000 people were killed. And despite being best known as a warrior he was also famed for his wildlife water-color paintings, which can fetch tens of millions of dollars to this day.

In addition to his acclaim as a hitter, Williams was a second lieutenant in World War II and flew combat missions. He also survived being shot down as a fighter pilot in the Korean War. And despite being best known as a baseball player, he was a champion sport fisherman as well. He is the only person to have been inducted into two sporting halls of fame, baseball and fishing.

At the end of his life, Musashi wrote *A Book of Five Rings,* which contains a lifetime of wisdom on training, dueling, and martial arts strategy. At the end of his life, Williams wrote *The Science of Hitting,* which contains a lifetime of distilled wisdom on training, hitting, and baseball strategy. Both books are perennial best sellers that have resonated with generations of readers because they contain profound life insights that go beyond the martial arts and baseball.

What might be most surprising is that neither book has much of a metaphysical tone. Today we frequently see samurai warriors depicted in movies as having a Zen detachment that allows them to function as superhuman instinctual killing machines. And we also frequently see baseball players depicted in movies as using their numerous personal superstitions and team rituals to overcome an "unfair" edge their opponent has gained. On the contrary, both books go deep into technique. And both books are also far ahead of their time in emphasizing repeatedly that a swordsman or hitter must go beyond technique and constantly practice and train, thinking themselves into the opponent's mind.

The teachings of both of these authors, who were the foremost experts in their fields, are very much in opposition to a refrain you will often hear today: *follow your gut*. There is also no direct mention in either book of anything like "use your instincts" or "don't think, just do." On the contrary, both Musashi and Williams emphasize the need to be disciplined enough to train continuously, to study the opponent in advance of the contest, and to be a careful observer of the overall situation in the moments before the competition to gain an edge. Musashi famously wrote, "Perception is strong and sight weak." Williams wrote, "It's a matter of being observant…. You watch a pitcher warm up…the observant guy will get the edge."

People who make a habit of "going with their gut" are in truth cutting corners. If your younger sister asked you for advice about some important matter in her life, like whether to become a stuntwoman or a lawyer, you would never tell her not to worry about it and "trust your instincts." You'd go in the other direction and would discuss all the pros and cons of both options, suggest other people she could speak with, and help her do some research.

Musashi challenged his readers to not just merely read or memorize or imitate his book, but to "study hard to absorb these things into your body." Williams was more direct in challenging his readers: "You certainly cannot go through the motions and be a great hitter. Not even a good hitter. It's the most difficult thing to do in sport."

## A Lion in the Shade

"Breaking through the surface my head is dizzy and flashes of light bounce around my skull. Completely limp from the effort, my arms tingle as I heave new life into my oxygen depleted body," wrote Carlos Eyles in his masterpiece on spearfishing, *The Last of the Bluewater Hunters*. "In an hour over fifteen hundred pounds of fish are cleaned.... Fires erupt into life around our camp.... A fiesta is in the making."

During the short window of time between your last adventure and the next one, be certain to replenish yourself. Feast with your companions. And then go off on your own and rest like a lion in the grassy shade.

Allow your body to relax. Allow your mind to empty itself of all concern. Allow your powers to regenerate themselves. Conserve the enormous vibrant energy building within you, and be ready to strike when the next opportunity appears. To the outside world, show calm confidence. Hear the monkeys above you chattering nervously from the safety of the trees. See the gazelles all around you leaping into a frightened sprint every time they hear a twig snap. You are a lion. That means you relax, out in the open, projecting a smoldering strength. Not doing or saying anything until it is time to either take action or move on.

When a running back is handed the ball, he can't just run full speed straight ahead. He has to wait until a hole develops between the defenders and then explode through it. Never make your move until the time is right for swift, decisive action. Never expend your mighty power prematurely. Never show off your strength or allow others to see how strong you truly are. Never react to the actions of others, no matter how irritating or insulting, unless doing so can help you accomplish your objectives. Never worry about whether others approve of your calm, patient inaction. Simply wait until opportunity presents itself, and then pounce with all your power.

Sometimes monkeys will hurl fruit husks down around you to impress one another. Sometimes a brave gazelle will saunter just out of your striking range to provoke you. Sometimes another lion will roar in order to test your reaction. The world is full of instigators with too much time on their hands who want to stand out and make a name for themselves by interfering with the plans of others. Avoid people who seek conflict and the opportunity to tear something down rather than build up something of their own.

Commit to forging good relationships to accomplish your objectives. Avoid making enemies, because battling them is a distracting waste of your precious energy and time. If for some reason you have a critic or an antagonist, challenge yourself to win them over to your side. It takes far less energy to convert an enemy to a friend than to spar endlessly.

Stay even-keeled during these interludes while you are recharging your powers and consolidating lessons learned from the last adventure as you prepare to embark on the next one. With time on your hands, you can become restless and your mood can suffer. Remain positive and channel your attention into the next opportunity. Learn how to keep yourself in a good mood, and forget how to be in a bad mood. Eat well and get plenty of rest. At night, as you drift off to sleep, don't allow yourself to twist and fidget grappling with deep questions like *What am I going to do next?* When you are drowsy and tired your mind is more adept at identifying problems than solutions. So learn how to relax, breathe deeply and fall asleep like a lion would on the savannah. If you wake up in the morning with your subconscious having handed you a solution, that's a gift from the heavens.

After a particularly successful adventure allow yourself additional time to decompress. As author, photographer, and elite freediver Carlos Eyles wrote, "The glow of the day keeps us up until well after midnight. There was magic in this day, and I refuse to yield to sleep, knowing how few of these moments there are in a lifetime."

## Change the World?

He was born in a backwater, and his father died while he was young. He proved to be excellent at riding horses, a brave soldier, and a successful general whose men followed him eagerly into battle. From his humble beginnings he rose quickly, and went on to become the father of a nation. Does that sound like George Washington, America's first president? Or is it a description of Genghis Khan, one of history's most merciless conquerors? Or both? Each of these men went down in history for facing enormous challenges and ultimately changed the world.

Many of today's young adults feel an unspoken pressure to be working on something—*right now*—that will change the world. But this assumes that changing the world is automatically a good thing. The example of Genghis Khan, who changed the world via unequalled conquest, destruction, enslavement, and killing, shows that it is not. Usually when people use the phrase *change the world*, what they really mean is *save the world*. That is an impulse that likely derives from so many movies where a lone cackling madman with some kind of doomsday machine holds the fate of the entire planet in his hands.

We don't need every single person on Earth trying to save the world from some kind of real or metaphorical time bomb as the clock ticks down to zero. What *is* needed is for each person to do their part—be it small or large—through a constructive mission informed by their adventures. While you are in the adventure stage, challenge yourself like Washington did in his youth so that you amass the self-knowledge that will eventually be needed to make a contribution to the world. Challenges, problems, and conflicts exist for your enjoyment and to educate you. So have successes and have failures. Fall in love and have breakups. Visit new places, and return to the ones you like and avoid the ones you don't. Life is nothing other than solving a series of problems along the path of your adventures for now, and ultimately along the mission path.

You don't have to single-handedly save our planet from annihilation by an asteroid or find a cure for cancer in order to be successful. "Success" is an elusive target because it is generally a measure of how impressive our outcomes are to other people rather than how we feel about them. Success is never the end of anything, because there is always more progress to be made. It doesn't matter if other people consider you a success as a result of the adventures you pursue. But it does matter whether your adventures enable you to learn and grow. If not, then why go through it all?

Many people who want to "change the world" are trying to overcome some kind of deeply painful episode from their formative years. Steve Jobs and Jeff Bezos were adopted. Bill Gates and Mark Zuckerberg had difficulty making friends. Alexander the Great, Julius Caesar, Genghis Kahn, and Hernando Cortez were sociopaths from today's point of view, with a lot in common with villains from the James Bond films.

Ayn Rand, the author of *The Fountainhead* and *Atlas Shrugged* said, "I decided to become a writer—not in order to save the world," but rather to create the kind of people and events she could respect and admire as examples for her readers. Her writing didn't save the world, but it changed the world for the better. And that is the point. Pursue your deeply personally important adventures, work, and mission. The underlying goal of each person's mission and legacy should be to leave the world a little better.

As the experiences you've gained in the adventure stage begin to coalesce, they will form the core of your mission. Your mission and work should do good, or they are not worthy of you. Making money is not a bad thing of course, but it is not heroic. A good starting point would be, "I'm going to pursue something that is personally important to me and does good, and my hope is that it ultimately unfolds into something important to others, and from there it may go on to change the world."

## Who am I?

"It's a show about nothing!" Jerry Seinfeld has often quipped, modestly brushing off having created *Seinfeld*, arguably the greatest television comedy of all time and having earned over a billion dollars from its production and syndication. *Seinfeld* fans know it is certainly not a show about nothing, but then what *is* it about?

For clues, we can look at how its intricately crafted episodes were created. According to urban legend, Seinfeld would get groups of young writers in a room to cough up all the most outlandish experiences they had as young adults in New York. From these seeds the multiple subplots of the episodes would germinate. Everything from being willingly emasculated by the Soup Nazi because his soup is so damn good, to entering Little Jerry in a cockfight in order to get off the 'bounced check wall of shame.' Every few years the writing staff was replenished with new young writers as the previous group of writers' story nuggets was depleted.

From that angle, we can see that *Seinfeld* is part of a great storytelling tradition: "Young adult goes to New York City to seek fortune, has amazing adventures against the backdrop of the world's most eccentric people, and along the way answers the question, *Who am I?*

Michael Lewis's *Liar's Poker* is also part of this rich tradition. In this biographical tale, Lewis lands his first job as a bond salesman for Salomon Brothers after majoring in history at Princeton. Lewis is appalled by his experiences among a band of obnoxious, juvenile hooligans. A number of his colleagues take advantage of their clients with no remorse, and in the end Salomon Brothers essentially implodes.

But perhaps the greatest example of the "new adult in New York" adventure story is Bud Fox in Oliver Stone's cautionary tale, *Wall Street*. Life as a stock broker is insufficiently glamorous for Bud, and he dreams of becoming like his idol, Gordon Gekko, the infamous Wall Street robber baron. Using his persistence and ingenuity, Bud schemes his way into becoming Gekko's protégé, but only at the price of offering up his father's company, Bluestar Airlines, as a target for Gekko's corporate-raider activities.

One evening, in his luxury Manhattan apartment, which has been purchased with ill-gotten gains from insider trading, Bud can't sleep. Next to him is Darien, essentially a high-class call girl and part-time interior decorator. Bud goes out onto the balcony and looks over the lights of the city. In a daze he asks aloud, "Who am I?" The problem for Bud is that he is looking to his unethical mentor, Gekko, for cues as to how to live his life. But we as viewers see he should really be turning to his salt-of-the-earth father.

Papa Fox would probably tell Bud something like, "I can't tell you who you are. But I do know that every person at their core wants to be great, to be loved, and to do something that matters to the world. And every person needs a mission to channel this drive. A person can be born with tremendous talents and be handed stacks of money, but without a mission that person is simply killing time, running around inventing errands for themself. *You will never know who you truly are until you choose your mission and carry it out.*"

After a stint in prison, Bud realized his mission was to be a company builder rather than profiteer, and he eventually became CEO of Bluestar Airlines. Michael Lewis realized through his adventures at Salomon that he had no interest in bonds. He went on to entertain and educate the world through his mission as a writer, finding the "hidden opportunity" in many sectors of the economy as detailed in *Moneyball*, *The Big Short*, *Flash Boys*, *Playing to Win*, and others.

The *Seinfeld* characters have no mission. They go from one adventure to the next, never progressing as people. Don't fall into that trap. Has the adventure stage provided the lessons and self-knowledge you need? Then it is time to move forward. It is time to formulate your mission.

## 2. CHOOSE MISSION

### The Mission

"You'll never make any money out of children's books," J. K. Rowling's literary agent told her before the first Harry Potter book was published. But Rowling didn't care. As a kid who grew up devouring Jane Austen and J. R. R. Tolkien books, becoming a professional writer was all she had ever dreamed of.

While riding a train, she suddenly had the idea of a boy who didn't know he was a wizard until he got to wizard school. From there, even though she was a single mom with an infant, unemployed and impoverished, Harry Potter became Rowling's mission. She filled a shoebox with notes and began writing every day at Nicolson's café, because she couldn't afford to heat her apartment. She never expected to make any money out of it, but the books and the movies they spawned were all blockbusters.

There is one thing you must never forget to do. Even if you were to accomplish many other things—wealth, fame, power—but you forget to do this one thing, you will never achieve your full potential. On the other hand, through the process of accomplishing just this one thing, you will be well on your way to lasting fulfillment. When you discover what this one thing is, you will have discovered your *mission*.

A person is at their best when they are pursuing a mission that is larger than themselves. At their core humans are hunters, and the hunt was humankind's first mission. The missions of people today are more complex and larger in scope and longer in duration than the missions of ancient times. But the skills and instincts of the hunter are there within every person—for you to draw upon and to aid you in discovering and executing your mission.

When a person commits to a mission that is truly aligned with who they are at their core, working toward that mission brings satisfaction and fulfillment. It feels as though much progress is being achieved with little effort. On the contrary, effort that takes a person away from their mission makes one feel sluggish and saps their energy. You are the only person who can carry out your unique mission. Nobody else can do it for you and you can't execute any other person's mission either.

Abraham Lincoln freed over 3.5 million American slaves by issuing the Emancipation Proclamation in 1862. It was his mission to keep the United States together during the Civil War and abolish slavery. As president he used every available power to prevent the country from splintering. His efforts to free African American slaves and oversee the Union military forces consumed him throughout almost his entire presidency.

It was the greatest moral crisis America has ever faced. Lincoln was in mental and physical anguish as he had the ultimate responsibility for sending tens of thousands of soldiers into battle to fight—not against a foreign enemy, but against their own countrymen. His leadership prevailed, and served as the groundwork for the 13th Amendment to the constitution, which formally ended slavery. He will forever be remembered as one of America's greatest presidents.

In recent times there has been a tendency toward confusing *mission* with *mission statement*. This often happens with schools and nonprofits that need to issue reports to a wide audience. A school's mission is to educate children even if its values (as described in its mission statement) include being inclusive and giving back to the community. A *mission* is specific and quantifiable, while *values* are broad and aspirational.

For Rowling, Lincoln, and many others described in this book, a deeply fulfilling life is one devoted to the ongoing evolution and achievement of a mission through continually changing external circumstances. The mission, as well as life itself, is nothing other than a series of problems and challenges, each greater than the last, which a person finds ways to solve as they proceed along their lifepath.

## Plan *Your* Mission

Suffering from a bad case of food poisoning during a trip to Russia, young Tom Ford dragged himself back to his hotel. He was miserable studying architecture and thought, *I knew I didn't want to do what I was doing, and all of a sudden, FASHION DESIGNER came into my head! It just came to me like a computer printout.* Ford went on to become the chief designer at Gucci and launched his Tom Ford luxury brand in 2005. He ultimately sold it to Estée Lauder in 2022 for $2.8 billion.

What would you like to have inscribed on your tombstone? Yes, you are young, and your tombstone is many years away. But even if just for a moment, give it some thought. How about:

- "He Carefully Avoided All Risks"
- "She had Many Great Ideas (but Didn't Act on Them)"
- "He Lived the Life His Parents Wanted"

You get the point. Your mission clarifies and channels your energy into an enduring goal—which must be *your* goal. It should be unique and personal to you, or you will never find the motivation needed to push it forward year after year.

Take the time, right now, to distill your mission down into a single sentence. For example: "I will invent a fabric for clothing that is indestructible." Or, "I will find a way for athletes to rehabilitate their knees without surgery." Or, "I will combine my love of opera singing and horror movies into a new entertainment genre." Once you have made your mission clear and definite by committing it to writing, you can evaluate it more easily and confirm that it is yours. Often the desire to solve a problem leads to a mission.

Is this *your* goal? It would be futile to try to accomplish a life mission that somebody else wants you to carry out. Or to pursue a mission to which you are only halfheartedly committed. To do that would be the same as trying to be another person. You are *you*, so you must pursue *your* mission.

It may be tempting, but don't put the initial planning of your mission off for later with the assumption that you have plenty of time for that after you "settle down." It is important to choose your mission and lay the groundwork for it now, before you start your family, so that it is *your* mission. Once you have a spouse and children, your obligations and the complexity of your life will increase exponentially. At that point it will become much more difficult to clearly distinguish your mission from your family's needs if you are not already in at least the early stages of executing it.

Ask yourself why you've chosen to carry out *this* mission. Be truthful with yourself about the answer(s): To become rich? To impress others? To become famous? To make my parents happy? To amass power? To prove somebody wrong?

Hopefully, the answer contains as many of the following as possible: Because it is my calling! Because it will allow me to help others! Because there's nothing else I can imagine doing with my life! Because it is a vehicle for contributing my talents to the world! Because it is my one true passion! Because it will solve a problem about which I care deeply! If you choose one or more of these as your answers, you will swim with the current rather than against it as you pursue and execute your mission.

Remember, if your mission involves trying to change or save the world that's wonderful. But you are under no obligation from anyone to save humanity singlehandedly. However, you are responsible for being a person of good character, trying to help the people around you, and doing good work. You should only try to change the world if it is your true calling. Plan *your* mission.

## The Final Question

"I've tried all sorts of jobs," wrote Carlos Eyles, "The more money I made, the bigger chunks it took out of me." There were so many questions to be answered. Should Eyles work in a white-collar or blue-collar job? Should he work as a salesman? Could he be fulfilled working a job that took him away from the ocean?

Eventually, he decided he had to walk away from it all. He spent a summer off the coast of Catalina Island, living on a borrowed boat that he repaired a little bit at a time in exchange for the use of it. He challenged himself to live solely through his first love, spearfishing. He traded the fish he caught—the elusive white seabass and other blue water giants—for the provisions he needed. This led to an epiphany: *I was born a hunter*. With his calling in focus, he penned his epic memoir, *Last of the Blue Water Hunters*.

Life starts off for everyone as a series of questions. As a child's life unfolds and they receive knowledge from their family, their teachers, and their own direct experience, they are confronted by continuous questions. Some are small, some are large, but all must be answered:

- How can I win love from my parents?
- How can I avoid suffering?
- To what activities should I devote my time?
- How can I compete with my peers?
- Why should I obey society's rules?

As a person grows older and gains skills and confidence, their thoughts move on to larger questions, including:

- Who am I?

- What is the nature of the universe?
- How can I live a good life?

It is the ongoing burden and joy of answering these questions that makes a person's life worth living. Over the years a person begins to realize that the smaller and more practical questions have been answered, and the larger, more philosophical questions that remain are all in some way connected. In this manner, each person's life ultimately distills down to a single great question that can form the backbone of their life's mission.

"At age ten, I had found my life's passion. I dedicated myself to becoming the best racecar driver in the world," wrote future racing champion, Danica Patrick. "From day one, I knew *this* was my calling, my destiny, my dream—and I knew that someday I would make it my dream come true."

Some lucky people, particularly athletes and artists, may realize at an early age what they love to do and what their mission will be. But most of us have to finish school, go through the adventure stage, and put in time being educated by the world. This process helps us learn what we want—or *need*—to do with our lives.

When Conrad Hilton was a young adult in New Mexico, he couldn't seem to put into motion his dream of owning a bank. His mother told him: "You'll have to find your own future, Connie. If you want to launch big ships you have to go where the water is deep." His mentor, Emmet Vaughn said: "Go to Texas, and you'll make your fortune." Suddenly, armed with this advice, Hilton felt vitally alive, thinking: *There was the challenge, the adventure. Could I go into Texas with $5,000 and make it grow?*

When a person asks *Who am I?*, what they are usually really asking is *What is my mission?* With the adventure stage completed, it is time to go beyond asking questions and choose your mission. Don't be backed into a profession or make your decisions based on financial rewards alone. Make certain you are committing your life to something larger than yourself that allows you to contribute your gifts to the world and makes you excited to wake up each day. In short, don't settle for an occupation. Find your mission.

## Mission Prototypes

"I went off to college like a sleepwalker, like a zombie," wrote William Deresiewicz, a former Yale professor, in his book *Excellent Sheep*. "College was the 'next thing.' You went to college, you studied something, and afterward you went on to the next thing, most probably some kind of graduate school. Up ahead were vaguely understood objectives: status, wealth, getting to the top—in a word, 'success.'" He is most likely exaggerating a bit to make a point, but there is a nugget of truth within. "Success" is a vague and elusive term. Most people would really like to have a calling, a mission, and fulfillment.

Moses spent 40 years leading his people through the desert and brought them to the Promised Land. Ponce de León searched the Americas relentlessly for the Fountain of Youth. Tiger Woods dreamed of surpassing Jack Nicklaus's 18 major championship golf wins. These are among some of the most well-known and concisely stated missions of all time.

When a person is young, their mission is often expressed in indistinct or nebulous terms. It then begins to gather focus and clarity as they take small steps that lead them forward. As the person confronts challenges and accumulates experience, their vague and amorphous mission will slowly evolve and become more defined. This process will continue over the course of one's life, and the mission will grow with the person.

These are some of the primary types of missions that can be found throughout history, myth, legend, and fiction:

- Save/lead one's people:     Winston Churchill, Golda Meier
- Quest or journey:     Ponce de León, Columbus

- Surpass an idol: Tiger Woods, Mia Hamm
- Conquest of land/people: Alexander, Hernando Cortes
- Achieve enlightenment: Buddha, Dalai Lama
- Be the best at a skill: Meryl Streep, Michael Jordan
- Scientific discovery: Isaac Newton, Marie Curie
- Build a business: Oprah Winfrey, Steve Jobs
- Accumulate wealth/power: Warren Buffett, Vladimir Putin
- Create a lifestyle: Martha Stewart, Jay-Z
- Tell stories: J. R. R. Tolkien, J. K. Rowling
- Artistic endeavor: Michelangelo, Pablo Picasso
- Writing/Philosophy: Confucius, Ayn Rand
- Revenge/Destruction: Adolf Hitler, Genghis Kahn
- Extend family dynasty: British Monarchy, Ford family

The mission itself is not etched in stone. Rather, underlying it is a core concept that over the course of one's life both unfolds and becomes more focused and larger in scope through its ever-evolving execution.

In reviewing the names in the list above one thing that is fairly constant, however, is that nearly all of these individuals put almost all of their adult energy into their mission. It was their primary passion, and the thing they loved most in life. The mission was not a part-time endeavor or something they would focus on for only periods of time. It was an all-consuming lifelong project, and from the outside looking in, some of the people listed here led spartan or meager lives.

Deresiewicz does an excellent job of defining a calling, which is the backbone of all missions: "It isn't something that you choose; it chooses you. It is the thing you can't *not* do.... But the summons doesn't happen by itself. You have to do the work to make yourself receptive to it." You first must free yourself of all the alternatives other people think you ought to care about.

## The Seductions of Laloki

"Flynn, you deserve to succeed, anyway—if only because you're too ignorant to know better," said the planters who came to visit Errol Flynn's thriving tobacco plantation along the Laloki River in colonial New Guinea.

After establishing the plantation, Flynn proudly watched the tobacco plants blossom. His native foreman and his tobacco workers knew how to grow the crop, and now Flynn could relax. Before long he fell in love with a local beauty, Tupersalai, and she came to live with him in his bamboo plantation home. Neither spoke the other's language, so they would go down to the river to swim every day. "I frolicked with Tupersalai by the riverbanks or lay with her in the soft sand at the shore," wrote Flynn. "Tupersalai and I drifted." Flynn lost interest in tobacco, his books, and in everything else as the months drifted by.

If resources were unlimited, there would be no need to struggle, strive, or compete. And if you obtained everything you needed without much effort, what would life be like? You could be living in a lush tropical paradise like Laloki, yet profoundly depressed, like Flynn became. If you achieved success but there was nobody to talk with to share your most intimate thoughts, your victories would likely feel hollow.

Life is a struggle. But in our modern world, advertisers and their celebrity spokespeople are constantly trying to convince us that the objective of our lives should be to do an end-run around this struggle and find a way to live a life of comfort, luxury, and consumption. But the reality is that there are no shortcuts. It is struggling toward goals that matter to us that leads to fulfillment, and it is pain-free fun and consumption that is hollow.

All the resources humans need to live—land, food, fuel—are "scarce resources." They are valuable, because they are limited in quantity. It is competition for scarce resources that drives both human life and the history of our species. Self-worth is derived by being productive, besting competitors, and by enjoying surplus resources with friends and loved ones.

The pursuit of a mission takes shape through competition for scarce resources and utilizing those resources to move the mission forward. Without scarce resources to quest after, competitors to outshine, and loved ones with whom to celebrate victories, no true missions could exist. Life would simply be survival.

In 1993, Michael Jordan held a press conference. He shocked the world by announcing he was retiring from basketball after having won three consecutive NBA championships. "I have nothing more to prove in basketball," Jordan said. "I have no more challenges."

Imagine having so much success at one of the most difficult professions in the world and making so much money doing it that you grew bored and depressed. After retiring, Jordan played Minor League Baseball for two years just to see how well he could do. He enjoyed being one of the guys rather than the star of the team. Baseball was his Laloki. And he might have remained there, but in 1994, there was a Major League Baseball strike. Phil Jackson and his teammates welcomed Jordan back to the Bulls, and they won three more titles together. He needed the strike to show him his true calling. Basketball greatness was his mission.

Flynn, too, was rescued from his depression in Laloki when a telegram arrived from Joel Swartz, the Hollywood producer he had taken up the Sepik River. Swartz asked Flynn to come to Tahiti to play a role in his new movie, *Wake of the Bounty*. Flynn parlayed this role into a career as a pirate, boxer, cowboy, Robin Hood, and many other swashbuckling roles in Hollywood movies. He had found his calling and true mission as an actor.

Fulfillment is the absence of depression. Depression is the absence of fulfillment. Do not seek a life of relaxation in paradise. That is a false choice. Seek your calling, and work hard every day at executing your mission.

### The Immortality Project

"There was an insane, terrifying roar, all the windows were shattered, and the scorched black silhouette of [11-year-old Giorgio Armani] emerged out of the smoke," wrote Renata Molho in *Being Armani*. The future fashion designer and his friends had been blowing things up with gunpowder. One boy died, and Giorgio was hospitalized for 40 excruciating days while his burns were treated. Afterward he became "an observer, timid, introverted, and keenly aware of everything going on around him."

As a boy Armani played with erector sets and became good at making things with his hands. He would buy items at the Milanese flea market, rebuilding and repairing them. His family didn't have much money, but his mother made stylish clothes for him out of old military uniforms and parachutes and sent him to school as well dressed as anyone. "Perhaps my love of sober, discreet, understated clothing came, subconsciously, out of that childhood memory," he said.

After a few years of military service, Armani was 24 and dabbling in photography. One of the models he photographed, his friend Rachele Enriquez, helped him get a job in the advertising department at La Rinascente, a successful Italian department store. "His gift for observation proved very useful." Before long he was put in charge of men's apparel and then was hired by Nino Cerruti to design men's clothing.

"Giorgio was growing both professionally and personally," wrote Molho. "He bought a secondhand Porsche convertible and let his hair grow long.... Already Armani was conceiving a softer, looser fashion, keyed to the spirit of modernity." Armani left Cerruti and launched the Giorgio

Armani company in 1975. His comfortable, minimalistic suits and trousers in neutral tones quickly began to sell well, particularly in America.

Building a company that made products with an aesthetic and quality Armani could tightly control was his mission, and over five decades he grew it into his own unique "immortality project." The term *immortality project* was coined in the 1970s by Ernest Becker, a German anthropologist. The essence of his theory is that:

- Every person develops unique "character armor" as a child based on influences of environment, parents, and core personality. These are thick layers of self-protective reflex reaction to the external world. They can never be shed or fully transcended as an adult.
- Unlike animals, every human being knows that life ultimately ends in death. The only way to avoid debilitating neurosis from knowing death awaits us is to create an immortality project for oneself that will live on after we die. This allows us to "cheat death."
- The key to depression-free life is to pick an immortality project (e.g., a mission) that synchs up with one's character armor. Each person's immortality project is highly individualized and specific to them.

Although he became as recognizable and famous as the Hollywood stars he dressed, Armani has continued to remain an introvert, rarely socializes, and prefers to focus on his work. Giorgio Armani is one of the last hugely successful fashion brands launched in the 1970s that has remained independent and is not part of a larger luxury conglomerate.

Childhood experiences mixed with self-knowledge from adventures give form to a person's mission. Some of the most fulfilling missions, like Armani's, become so by growing into immortality projects (and later become a legacy). "No other fashion designer, with the possible exception of Ralph Lauren, was so determined to articulate a specific way of life," Molho wrote. "Armani, working with the same stubborn determination he had shown since he was very young, was pursuing a goal: His ambition was to build and convey a universe of [symbols] that express him and that represent him."

## Distractions Are "Termites"

"*Dancing with the Stars* has reached out to me, and so has *Maxim* magazine, for a photo shoot that I'm pretty sure would've had much more to do with skin than soccer," said Olympic gold medalist and World Cup champion, Carli Lloyd. "I have a brand. You know what it is? Soccer player. It's the only brand I have any interest in."

When Lloyd's trainer, James Galanis, helped her create a mission plan that would eventually culminate in her becoming the top soccer player in the world, he told her, "Soccer needs to be number one in your life. Not your boyfriend or your social life or anything else. Soccer."

There is a hedge fund with a simple method for determining when a company will go from being very successful to falling off a cliff into terrible performance. They have one of their analysts track how the CEOs of publicly traded companies spend their personal time. If one of those CEOs purchases a yacht or any other time-consuming toy, or becomes a triathlete or takes up any other time-consuming hobby, the hedge fund immediately bets against that CEO's company. They assume those CEOs will become distracted.

When you are truly engrossed in and motivated by your mission, the universe rolls out the red carpet and gives you opportunities to push your mission forward and succeed. Alternatively, when you are distracted by some toy you want or some other activity you wish you were doing, the universe plants chomping termites under the floorboards of your mission.

When you aren't fully engaged with, focused on, and absorbed by your mission, you have to allocate resources to both the mission and side pleasures. But when your progress on the mission provides you all the fulfillment and enjoyment you could ever desire, then there is no resources conflict or allocation decision to make.

Ted Williams, who accomplished his mission of becoming the greatest hitter who ever lived said, "I treated my bats like they were special. I didn't want them chipped or discolored, because those are distractions. I cleaned my bats with alcohol every night. I took them to the post office to check their weights." Williams also ensured his uniforms fit perfectly as well so those, too, did not distract him while batting.

Here are some keys to avoiding distraction during the mission stage:

- Make certain to have true all-in adventures during the adventure stage of life. This is often the root cause of distraction during later life stages (e.g., a "midlife crisis" resulting from the need to pursue the adventures you missed out on while you were young).

- In order to accomplish your life mission, you need a breakthrough. Breakthroughs don't come from doing several things. They come from immersing yourself in your area of focus and pursuing it exclusively like an elite athlete or a monk.

- Amassing collections of things takes a lot of energy. Do you really need to own ten cars or three homes at the same time? Are you collecting primarily to experience the thrill of the hunt? If you feel compelled to collect, try to figure out why.

- When you have financial success, avoid ratcheting up your standard of living so that you have to keep earning more and more to feed the hungry beast of your lifestyle. Pour your energy into your mission, not into ever more expensive homes, clubs, and habits.

The confusion of artifacts (homes, cars, toys) and activities (hobbies, collecting, illicit endeavors) with mission is the noise that can make the execution of a great and fulfilling life difficult. Like Lloyd and Williams, be focused and meticulous and leave nothing to chance. Choose the mission that commands your full and complete attention.

## The Mission Is a Project

It was a massive 12,000-pound, 17-foot-high block of marble that had been brought to Florence fifty years earlier. Two famous Italian sculptors had each tried to bring it to life as a King David statue, but each had failed due to its enormous size and brittleness. Now, in the year 1499, the partially carved block had been untouched for over two decades. The Wool Guild and Opera Authority were responsible for the upkeep and decoration of the cathedral. They had grown increasingly concerned about the substantial investment they had made in this huge block. Although they interviewed Leonardo da Vinci and other highly regarded artists, it was 26-year-old Michelangelo Buonaroti who convinced them to give him the commission to complete the statue.

Michelangelo had recently completed his first great sculpture in Rome, the Pieta. Now he returned to Florence, which was considered the center of the world for fine art. It was there that he could advance his mission, which was to become the greatest artist of all time. He would carry out this mission, one project at a time. And the David would ultimately become his greatest project and known as the finest sculpture in the world.

Stated in the simplest terms, *projects* are "temporary mobilizations of resources that produce a deliverable." Your life mission is a massive undertaking. So like Michelangelo, it can be useful to conceptualize your mission as a series of projects. And in turn, the mission itself can be viewed and planned as a single overarching project.

First, he created a miniature wax model of the statue he planned to carve. He had to be meticulous with his engineering. The statue would be mounted high above the ground and needed to balance on its two legs, but he was constrained by the cuts the previous sculptors had already made in the marble. Michelangelo would submerge his wax model in a tank of water and allow it to rise out of the water little by little. That way, he could visualize each horizontal layer he had to release from the block with his carving tools. It was an excruciatingly difficult project, both mentally and physically. He hardly ate or slept, and when he did sleep, it was in his clothes.

Project managers have the responsibility for planning their projects, organizing the resources needed, overseeing the execution of the work, and delivering the final output on schedule. They organize their work according to generally agreed upon project management principles:

- Projects consist of three phases: *planning, execution, and closing*. Each phase is divided into milestones, consisting of a defined portion of the work to be completed within a set amount of time. This allows the project manager to measure and track progress.

- The execution of every project is also subject to three limitations: *budget, scope of work, and schedule*. Each of these is a variable that affects the other two (e.g., if a project falls behind schedule, the budget has to be increased or the scope has to be reduced).

- Ultimately, the key to a successful project is a *detailed plan* that encompasses every contingency, a *compelling vision* that your helpers can clearly understand and find motivating, and a *realistic deadline* you consistently work toward with achievable milestones.

You only have one mission, but you'll also have projects along your lifepath that are subordinate to the mission. Buying a home. Helping a loved one recover from an illness. Coaching your kid's team for a season.

In carrying out a project that is important to your mission, it can be very helpful to emulate Michelangelo and his wax model. Start small and figure out the problems before you go to work with your hammers and chisels. As problems "emerge from the water tank," always remind yourself that every problem has a solution.

**The Mission Is a Work of Art**

Michelangelo was reportedly prone to "fits of perfection," which is another way of saying he was what we might consider today a "tortured artist." He strenuously resisted feedback from his teachers early in life and from his clients later in life. And his nose was permanently disfigured by a blow from a fellow sculptor during an argument.

His genius as an artist is clearly evident in the groundbreaking composition of his David statue. The norms of his time were to present David in the moment *after* his victory over Goliath with a sword in hand and Goliath's head at his feet. But Michelangelo went in a completely different direction. He showed David in the moments *before* the confrontation, in a naturalistic relaxed pose with his weight on one leg and a sling in hand. He also broke with the traditions of his fellow Renaissance artists who always sculpted or painted human figures with clothing, due to pressures from the Catholic church. The David was the first large scale fully nude statue sculpted since the antiquity of Greek and Roman times.

Stated in the simplest terms, *art* is "an expression of an artist's imaginative and conceptual ideas intended to be appreciated for their beauty and emotional power." Your life mission is a multifaceted expression of your ideas too. So, like Michelangelo, it can be useful to conceptualize your mission as a series of artworks. And, in turn, the mission itself can be composed and executed as a single overarching work of art.

The execution of the David, which took Michelangelo two years to carve, also displayed his incredible perfectionism. He had to work around the miscalculations of the previous sculptors who had worked the gargantuan marble block, which is likely why the figure he carved is shown in a relaxed, leaning pose. He blended their errors into his art. He turned their mistakes into an unparalleled work of near perfection, from the curve of David's spine to the veins showing on the surface of his skin.

Like Michelangelo, the artists we think of as the greats are those who both go beyond the conventions of their time and find ways to turn imperfections in their available resources into a beautiful completed work. These skills and this mindset also apply to the execution of a person's life mission.

Artists are creative people who imagine and produce works that are interesting and beautiful in order to bring pleasure and enjoyment to themselves and others. Different types of artists have various technical skills – sculptors, painters, actors, musicians – but they also share a common creative process:

- Artists have to be able to put themselves in a *creative mood*. It is difficult to force oneself to produce art when upset or distracted.

- During an initial *idea-collection stage*, an artist allows various ideas to flow spontaneously into their mind and retains the best ideas.

- Art reflects the life and feelings of the artist. At the start of the execution of the idea, *the artist infuses themselves* into the art.

- After the production of the art is underway, artists lose themselves in their art and *become one with the work*.

- Bad brushstrokes and offkey notes are to be expected. The artist *blends these mistakes* into the finished work to make it an original.

In producing the smaller works of art that make up the larger artwork that is your life mission, it can be helpful to emulate Michelangelo and his flawed block of marble. The greatest artists are able to start from the position of solving a problem. They can turn both the problem and their own unique ideas over and over in their mind until the creative inspiration is found to produce something groundbreaking and beautiful.

## Create Your Own World

We've all seen tricked-out, ultracool "man caves." Well, after working as a fashion model and then as one of the first female stockbrokers—and before becoming a billionaire through taking her lifestyle company public—Martha Stewart created a "woman cave" for herself. She launched a catering business out of the basement of Turkey Hill, her home in Westport, Connecticut. The house was ideal, because the thick early-19th-century stone walls kept everything cool. She had a commercial stove with two ovens, a refrigerator, and "lots and lots of butcher-block countertops on which to work."

People with a special mission need a private base of operations. A place where they can refine their plans and test their ideas, house their equipment and mementos, and meet with their colleagues to strategize. Chefs have commercial kitchens. Martial artists have dojos. Artists have studios. Scientists and inventors have laboratories. Silicon Valley entrepreneurs have garages. Professional athletes have gyms for working out and "me-rooms" to house their trophies. Celebrities have private islands like Brando's Tetiaroa in French Polynesia and Richard Branson's Necker Island in the Caribbean. And, of course, supervillains have lairs.

With such an important mission—keeping all of humanity safe—Superman has an equally important personal sanctuary, the Fortress of Solitude, hidden in the Arctic. It was built from giant clear crystals using the advanced architecture of the Man of Steel's long-dead home planet, Krypton. And Batman too has a refuge that reflects his personality: The Batcave, a series of caverns under his alter ego Bruce Wayne's mansion—gloomy, dark, wet, and concealed by a waterfall—housing the Batmobile, Batjet, and other high-performance vehicles in hangars. It contains mechanical workshops, a gymnasium, and a variety of Batsuits, gear, and trophies from Batman's adventures.

When you choose your life mission, *you* set the rules and can set up your base of operations however you want. You get to create a world whose resources you control. In 1945, after World War II ended, Ferdinand Porsche began production of the Porsche 365 in the wooden sheds of a former sawmill in Austria. Forty-nine air-cooled 365s were built by hand, and that artisanal tradition is retained in Porsche's DNA to this day.

When he started his business, Giorgio Armani worked from a design studio that was barely twelve feet square. He had furnished it with "nothing but a few wicker chairs set around a huge worktable that was used interchangeably for long business meetings, press conferences, and frugal meals." From that diminutive but effective space, Armani revolutionized men's fashion.

Create your own little world. Make it a place that puts you in a constructive frame of mind, not a pristine museum where you're afraid to touch anything. Set it up so you're proud when people come to visit. Have your own style that is unique to you. Superman builds everything out of crystals. Batman likes to paint everything black.

Once you have created your base of operations don't fall into the trap of always trying to expand and make it more elaborate. The bigger you try to grow it, the greater the odds become that it will require a lot of maintenance, compromises, and bureaucracy. You want your base of operations to remain unique to you and support your mission. You don't want it to become a financial drain or otherwise divert your energy from your mission. Martha Stewart's catering business was profitable from day one due to the low cost of operating out of her Turkey Hill basement. She said, "Create a frugal culture. Not cheap, but frugal...waste of any kind really bothers me."

Live the life you want on a scale that you can manage and keep it consistent with your vision and values. Envision and create a world and lifestyle uniquely tailored to you, and enjoy it every day.

## Purposeful Addiction

Siddhartha seated himself beneath the Bodhi Tree in the meditation posture and vowed not to rise from meditation until he had attained perfect enlightenment. He had already been focused single-pointedly for six years, meditating on the ultimate nature of all phenomena, and realized he was close to attaining full enlightenment. Now, as demons tried to distract and tempt him, he perceived their weapons to be fragrant flowers and deepened his concentration. He continued on, and at dawn the final veils of ignorance were lifted from his mind. In the next moment he became a *Buddha*, a fully enlightened being.

When most people hear the word *addiction*, they consider it a negative or disparaging word. They might picture in their mind's eye an emaciated drug addict in dirty clothes, panhandling for change and sleeping in an alley. But another way to think of it is "losing yourself in something."

Have you noticed that when you have friends who are really passionate about an activity—be it restoring vintage motorcycles, competing in pickleball, designing jewelry, playing the guitar, or hang gliding—they will absolutely wear themselves out doing it? They will do it all day long if they can. They may forget to eat and sleep because they love doing it so much and are completely obsessed. They keep on going until they crash from exhaustion and then wake up and do it again.

This concept of losing yourself in something is also often portrayed in biographical books and movies that explore the extremes of human life. For example, soldiers fighting in a war will do anything for their unit and sacrifice themselves for their buddies. Athletes preparing for a championship run will push their bodies to the breaking point and beyond. A hospitalized patient with a terminal illness will immerse herself completely in seeking experimental therapies and alternative medicines. And an inmate who has been falsely imprisoned will put all of his waking hours into devising scheme after scheme to try to outwit his captors and escape.

Everyone is addicted to something, because ultimately everyone is looking to transcend their current situation. But most people let their addictions choose them. You absolutely want to avoid being addicted to anything illegal or immoral, particularly any mind-altering substances that can cause you physiological harm or take you in a downward spiral through making poor decisions. People go to gyms or nightclubs or chop firewood or go on long walks because they need release from the relentless grind of daily life. Make certain you find a constructive way to defuse these normal and recurring tensions.

To have a destructive addiction is to be out of control and to give up choice. On the other hand, to have a *purposeful addiction* is to embrace an objective larger than yourself and be governed by your own choices. The human species makes quantum leaps through people's purposeful addictions. Think of the Buddha meditating with extreme concentration and focus for years until he experienced enlightenment. Think of Isaac Newton laboring for years over his calculations until he devised his laws of motion. Think of the Wright brothers undertaking experiment after experiment and ultimately unraveling the fundamentals of powered flight. Purposeful addiction is a mission taken to its limit.

You have to go deep for a sustained period of time, dedicate yourself, and experience hardships if you want to make significant and transcendent breakthroughs. You can't simply dabble in any pursuit in which you hope to achieve greatness. You have to allow it to become an addiction.

Avoid destructive addictions, including overdoing it with alcohol and social media. Consciously choose positive and purposeful addictions. Rather than "follow your passion," instead "choose your addiction." Choose to be addicted to good health, learning through your adventures, and ultimately to your family and to your mission.

## Extraordinarily Thick Skin

According to urban legend, a reporter once criticized Van Halen lead singer, David Lee Roth, for only being able to write songs about girls and cars. An offended Roth quickly replied, "As a matter of fact, we've never done a song about cars, but thanks, that's a great idea!" The release of Van Halen's next album, *1984*, led with *Panama*, a debauched song about a 1950s Buick, which quickly became their greatest hit up until that point. The multiplatinum album completed the culmination of Van Halen's mission to become the biggest rock band in the world.

You have to push your mission forward simply because it is your calling and you believe in it. You can't choose your mission based on being fashionable or seeking public admiration. And you can't be the judge of whether your mission is good or valuable to the world. It is up to others to choose whether to admire you and to determine whether your mission is a good one. It takes a thick skin to put in all the hard work that goes with your life mission and then leave it to the world to be the ultimate evaluator.

Nicolaus Copernicus, the Polish astronomer, was convinced the earth orbits around the sun. During his lifetime (1473–1543), the academic world and Catholic Church believed the opposite, that the sun revolves around the earth. At the age of forty, not wishing to arouse anger from the Church, he distributed a manuscript describing his ideas to a few close friends. He spent the next twenty years making the calculations necessary to turn his manuscript into a book. He was wary of ridicule or running afoul of the Church and held back from publishing the book until the very end of his life. He received the book from the printer the day he died, at seventy years old, never to see his ideas proven true or gain mass acceptance.

Italian astronomer Galileo Galilei, was born twenty-one years later, in 1564. He built one of the world's first telescopes and used it to make astrological observations that were far more accurate than ever before. It was obvious to him that Copernicus was correct, and he began announcing his discoveries to the world without worrying about the consequences. The Church was still opposed to the idea that the earth is not the center of the universe and ordered Galileo to cease spreading the idea of the heliocentric solar system. He spent the next six years writing a book laying out the evidence that Copernicus had been right. He published it, which angered the Church, and he was brought to trial before the Inquisition. He was put under house arrest, but even then, he still continued his work.

Ultimately, Galileo was responsible for convincing the world that the planets revolve around the sun. Galileo is one of history's most preeminent examples of a person having both a deep conviction in their ideas and an extraordinarily thick skin. He was ahead of his time, and his ideas were groundbreaking. He believed in them so firmly he was willing to pay a significant price to bring his ideas to the attention of the world.

The price of doing great work is that you have to put it out into the world so that it can be evaluated, and so that you can obtain useful feedback to improve it. You have to expect criticism if your life mission upends an established way of looking at or doing things. If you are breaking new ground you must anticipate resistance even if you know, like Galileo did, that you are right. In fact, if you are not being criticized or second-guessed, your mission is probably not big enough. A new and novel message is not going to be instantly accepted at face value. It takes a thick skin to pursue a life mission whose importance is obvious to you but not to others.

Resist the impulse to lash out every time you or your mission are criticized. Reacting poorly to criticisms isn't strength; being overly sensitive shows weakness and a lack of confidence. Learn how to win over critics with reason, persuasion, proof, and humor. Learn not just how to weather setbacks, but how to absorb them, get something useful out of them, and keep on going. Or as Van Halen's Roth sang in "Jump," another huge hit from *1984*, "You've got to roll with the punches to get to what's real."

## Life as a Wrestling Match

"He looked at the granite. To be cut, he thought, and made into walls. These rocks are here for me; waiting to be split, ripped, pounded, reborn; waiting for the shape my hands will give them." These were the thoughts Ayn Rand articulated in 1943's *The Fountainhead* through her greatest character, red-haired, jackhammer-wielding architect Howard Roark, whose mission was to transform the way people use buildings. "He liked the work. He felt at times as if it were a match of wrestling between his muscles and the granite."

We sometimes forget that life is a wrestling match. A great many people today have come to expect every aspect of life to be perfect and hassle-free. And they often seem to be on the lookout for people to blame when it isn't. Decide instead to look for evidence that right now is the best time ever in the history of the world to be alive. Seek evidence that everything in your life, including the challenges you face, is exactly as it is meant to be. Choose to embrace the struggle.

Tech visionary Elon Musk isn't running away from stress or struggle. He pursues and embraces it. It is almost as though he pays a staff of writers to top one another with tall tales about how extreme a life he is living:

*Elon works seven days a week.... Elon sleeps on the floor of his office.... Elon has decided to scale back his weekly work hours to only 80.... Elon has no time for friends or socializing.... Elon's life is out of balance.... Elon works on weekends and during vacations.... Elon doesn't exercise.... Elon breaks his days down into five-minute increments.... Elon would give up eating if he could.... Elon has no life outside work.... Elon is giving up all personal* *possessions.... Elon is moving all his companies to Texas.... Elon is buying Twitter for $44 billion....*

Yet Musk seems to love his life and everything he is doing. He is apparently willing to give up personal comfort and undergo enormous struggles in order to make his Tesla electric cars and SpaceX rockets and his other companies and inventions truly great. He knows that whatever he puts tremendous effort into will give him tremendous fulfillment in return.

Sometimes you will hear people "humble-bragging," competing over who has the busier schedule or who is under more stress. But if we are experiencing busyness and stress as a consequence of carrying out our mission, that is something we have voluntarily signed up for and should therefore embrace. None of us can or should try to shield ourselves from stress or doing hard things. We need some kind of daily struggle toward meaningful objectives, like a life mission, in order to know we are alive.

You are pursuing your life mission because it is deeply important to you. And having a deeply important objective that is just out of reach at the moment is highly beneficial to you in many ways. Stress and struggle, and the cycle of setbacks and triumphs, educate your mind and help you increase your capabilities.

When you first embark on your mission, for a while you'll be Forest Gump on the shrimp boat, hauling up nothing but toilet seats and old beer cans in your nets. But then some combination of hard work, prayer, and good karma will take you forward and lead to nets overflowing with shrimp. Everyone who executes a great mission has a lot of ups and some downs. The downs are where persistence and grit come in. Execution of a life mission follows a pattern: things going well, punctuated by a crisis that has to be resolved. When the crisis hits, don't overreact. Take some time and think, *Where's the hidden opportunity in this?*

In the evening, Roark "lay in the tub for a long time and let the cool water soak the stone dust out of his skin.... The greatness of the weariness was its own relief: It allowed no sensation but the slow pleasure of the tension leaving his muscles." Struggle is a key ingredient of deep fulfillment.

### Let the Mission Unfold

"A director is the man who presides over divine accidents," said Orson Welles. He was the director, writer, producer, and star of *Citizen Kane*, considered by many to be the greatest motion picture ever made. His point is that you start with a vision for a movie and a script you plan to follow. But great directors realize the movie has a life of its own that is larger than the people making it. Directing a movie requires capturing all the serendipitous material during filming that is even better and more magical than what was envisioned in the script.

Similarly, Clausewitz, the Prussian general who is considered by some to be the greatest military strategist of all time, said something to the effect that *a battle plan is only intended to last until the first contact with the enemy*, and then a general has to be willing to throw away the plan and seize the fortuitous opportunities that present themselves.

For any serious undertaking, you must have a written plan. Directors have screenplays. Generals have battle plans. But a director or general has to allow their plan the leeway and flexibility to benefit from lucky breaks and unexpected opportunities. The same is true of your mission. Have a mission plan so you know your objective and how you expect to accomplish it. But don't make it overly detailed or let yourself think there is only one set of steps you can take that will bring your mission to fruition. Allow yourself many paths forward, and allow fortuitous external circumstances to help you.

As you pursue your life mission you will likely have a tendency to want to make continuous, consistent, orderly progress toward your ultimate objective. But that would only be possible if everything in the world around us were constant and knowable, which we know to be the rarest of rarities. As you work toward incremental goals during the execution of your mission, you'll experience setbacks or make huge leaps forward due to the weather, changes in the economy, help or opposition from people along the way, or countless other variables.

Before Shawn Carter—better known as Jay-Z—became, in his own words, "the Michael Jordan of recordin'" and "the black Warren Buffett," he was a young adult being mentored by Jaz-O, a rapper four years his senior. Jay-Z learned from his mentor that his mission was not merely to be a rapper, but to turn himself into a brand. He pooled his resources with Damon Dash, and they founded Roc-A-Fella Records. Before long Jay-Z had seven platinum albums and a Grammy Award, and his Rocawear clothing line was pulling in $80 million per year through clever licensing deals. Then he retired from performing, became CEO of Def Jam Records and built it into a juggernaut through signing artists. He built a champagne brand now worth over $500 million, bought part of an NBA team, married Beyoncé Knowles, released another seven number one albums, outgrossed the Rolling Stones as a performer, created a sports management agency that turns athletes into brands, and launched a venture capital fund.

Through capitalizing on these organic and serendipitous endeavors, Jay-Z accomplished his goal of becoming a diversified global lifestyle brand like Oprah Winfrey or Martha Stewart. Let your mission become what it wants to become. There are a lot of roads that lead to the top of a mountain.

It is sometimes difficult to know if a setback is really a setback, or if it is actually aiding your mission in ways that haven't become clear yet. While you are in the middle of carrying out your mission, it can look at times like your plans are in disarray and everything is a total disaster. But later, when you can look back on what you accomplished, you can see that it all led to a great masterpiece like *Citizen Kane*.

When things look bleak, always remind yourself, "I'm exactly where I want to be right now. I'm proud of everything I've accomplished in the past, and I'm motivated by my plan that will take me forward into a bright future."

## You're a Professional

Joe Montana was considered too small to be an NFL quarterback. Jerry Rice was considered too slow to be an NFL wide receiver. But Bill Walsh, head coach of the San Francisco 49ers, saw something special and drafted each of them. Neither was the best *athlete* at their position in the NFL. But Walsh recruited them for their potential to be standout *professional* football players. Through their professionalism, Montana and Rice combined to lead the 49ers to three Super Bowl wins. And each won one more without the other, meaning that the two superstars were keys to each of the franchise's five Super Bowl victories.

Whatever life mission you choose, view yourself as a professional in everything you do to execute it, not an amateur. An amateur does something to the best of their abilities but the results they produce and their reactions to adversity can be inconsistent, because they are doing it as a pastime or a hobby. Your mission isn't a pastime. Handle all aspects of your mission with the same ethos a professional brings to their endeavors.

A professional has made a commitment to perform at the top level of skill and performance at their chosen activity and be paid for doing so. A professional knows how to train and prepare so as to always be in a position in which the odds favor success. A professional knows how to control their emotions. A professional knows how to execute when tired. A professional knows how to maintain focus when it matters most. A professional knows how to perform their role and help team members perform theirs. A professional knows how to keep composure under pressure. And, above all, a professional takes a much greater degree of responsibility and accountability for the outcomes they produce than an amateur.

Imagine interviewing an NFL quarterback going into a playoff game. Or a neurosurgeon before brain surgery. Or a commercial pilot about to fly 400 people across the Pacific during storm season. If you ask any of these professionals if they are worried, they will probably say something like: *No, I'm not worried, because I'm a professional. Every day when I do my job, I expect to encounter challenges and face new difficulties. I'm paid to keep my composure and find solutions.*

After throwing the winning pass, saving the patient's life, or landing the plane safely by avoiding a typhoon, a professional doesn't jump up and down, pump their fists and shout excessively about their success. They've been there before. So they express their appreciation to their teammates or crew, move on, and begin preparing for the next game, operation, or flight.

To be a professional in any field is very hard work and all-consuming. You won't find someone, for example, working simultaneously as an architect and a lawyer. A few of the world's top athletes, like Bo Jackson and Deion Sanders, were professional football players and professional baseball players at the same time, but couldn't sustain it very long. You have to dedicate your life to accumulating the specific mission skills and knowledge you need. That is how you become a professional in carrying out your mission.

"If you're a racer, you can't just have one great race. That's what separates the great racers from the amateurs. Mario Andretti...doesn't have bad races," said Paul Newman, who won an Oscar as an actor and a Le Mans championship as racecar driver. "[A] great driver's excellence is always there, can be tapped each and every day." Newman became a successful racer late in life after accomplishing his mission of becoming a great actor.

Becoming a professional at anything, including the execution of a life mission, brings with it tremendous pride and satisfaction. The deeper you go into any activity you care about, the more you appreciate it. As a person carrying out a mission, ideally you will develop the ethos of a professional and view your field of endeavor as the most challenging, exciting, interesting, satisfying, and rewarding thing you could have chosen to do with your life.

## Keep the Momentum Going

"A lot of people thought we were finished as a band, so it was surprising in itself that *Back in Black* came out at all," said Angus Young, lead guitarist of rock band AC/DC in an interview with *Vulture*. "When we were making it, it was a do-or-die effort. We figured, if it was our last album, let's make it a damn good one. I remember the record label going, 'The situation is bad enough as it is, and you want to cover the album in black, too?'"

The up-and-coming Australian band had just finished the *Highway to Hell* tour when flamboyant, hard-partying lead singer, Bon Scott, was found dead in a parked car, a victim of alcohol poisoning. The band was a tight-knit group of close friends who were trying to conquer the world together, and they were devastated and depressed. During funeral services, Scott's father, though grief-stricken, told the band they would have to find another singer and keep going, because Scott would have wanted it that way.

When you are in your prime, making good progress on your life mission and at the height of your game, maintaining combustion is effortless. One success ignites the next. But if you take the combustion or momentum you've gathered for granted, the flame can go out. Carelessness can allow the fire of your mission to go cold. Reigniting success and regaining your momentum isn't easy—like a pair of cold, clumsy hands searching for kindling and fiddling with matches.

Always keep the momentum going, no matter how well—or poorly—things are going with executing the mission. Even if you don't slack off, someone is always doing something either intentionally or inadvertently to gum up your progress. It is your job to prevent these buckets of water from dousing your fire. Success is never final. There's always breakfast tomorrow morning to be cooked, so it is up to you to keep the embers glowing.

The best way to prevent your momentum from stalling or your combustion from dwindling is to always position yourself to stay ahead. If you are playing ice hockey and you skate right to where the puck is, the odds are high that you will be skating right into an opponent or teammate and will have to come to a stop. Wayne Gretzky, the greatest scorer in NHL history, was well known for always skating to where the puck would end up and beating everyone to get there. In other words, keep the momentum going by anticipating rather than reacting. Work ahead of the situation.

"Nassau wasn't all white beaches. It was pissing down, there was flooding, and the electricity was out," Young said of recording *Back in Black*. "We'd sit through the night with a couple bottles of rum with coconut milk in and work." Incredibly, Scott had once told the band in jest that if they ever needed to replace him, they should consider a brilliant Scottish singer named Brian Johnson. So AC/DC tracked him down and were now recording with him in the Caribbean to honor Scott and his father's wishes.

Johnson heard the roaring thunder outside the studio and it inspired the first track, "Hells Bells." And one after the other, more amazing songs flowed from there. To this day, when you hear the *Back in Black* album, the energy—the momentum—of those sessions is sealed into the recordings for all time.

In memoriam to Scott, the band demanded an all-black cover for *Back in Black*. It remains the second-highest selling rock album of all time after Michael Jackson's *Thriller*. And it propelled AC/DC into superstardom.

Reigniting a fire from dead embers takes a lot of time. Getting your momentum going again from a standstill takes a lot of effort. But sustaining your mission by keeping it going at all times, thinking ahead, and taking nothing for granted will give you comfort. Once your mission is set, don't coast. Exhaust yourself every day pushing it forward. No food is as delicious, no rum with coconut milk as intoxicating, no sleep as deep as that after a hard day pushing the mission boulder up the mountain.

## The Ultimate Price

Heroes from movies and on television—James Bond, Charlie's Angels, Iron Man, Wonder Woman—seem at a superficial glance to represent a glamorous ideal version of life. But if we examine these characters more closely, we discover they are workaholics with no hobbies or personal life, no spouse or children. They don't care about anything but pursuing their mission of ridding the world of evil.

And that is fine. It makes sense. Provided we view these characters as occupying the early years of the mission stage of life. That is, they've already completed the adventure stage, and during those years obtained the skills and knowledge and motivations they needed to prepare themselves for their mission of crime fighting. And they have not yet started the family stage, during which they will need to spend more time meeting their obligations to others in their personal life.

In his Bond novels, author Ian Fleming was very clear that a secret agent like Bond could not go on indefinitely. He and his secret-agent peers would only have the luck and the vigor to face the physical dangers and mental stresses of confronting the world's greatest criminals for about ten years. Thereafter they'd presumably be deceased, physically or mentally disabled, or transition to fighting crime from a desk. (Surely, he didn't envision Hollywood keeping Bond alive for six decades—and counting!)

There's a saying that goes, "If you want the ultimate, you've got to be willing to pay the ultimate price." We admire these heroes we grew up with, because they are operating from a window of time in their lives during which they are willing and able to pay any price and take any risk necessary to carry out their mission. In achieving your life mission, it is important that you too recognize that the period between the end of the adventure stage of life and the beginning of the family stage is a crucial one. It is during this time that you have the latitude to devote yourself and your time fully to setting up your mission and pushing it forward so that it gains traction and momentum, takes form, and becomes established. It is during this window that you are most able to take financial and physical risks without potentially severe repercussions for your spouse and young children.

"The ultimate price" may be too singular a concept. The point is that committing fully to your mission, which you are most able to do during this brief and opportune stage in your life, comes with a high price. You have to be willing to devote all your time to your mission. You have to be willing to devote all your financial and other resources to your mission. You may have to risk your health and sanity at certain times in pursuing your mission. You will have to carry out many tasks that you don't want to do because you are both the "chief cook and bottle washer" of your mission.

And even more important than what you put in, there is much you will have to give up. Forget about sleeping in on weekends. Forget about spur-of-the-moment vacations. Forget about buying fancy cars and other toys. Forget about frequent partying with your friends. Are you willing to trade these things in exchange for the accomplishment of your mission?

Hopefully your answer is an emphatic, "*YES.*" Yes, you'll make this trade because nobody can accomplish your mission but you. Yes, you'll put in the hard work and stay disciplined because to do big things and become great comes with a price. Yes, you'll pursue this difficult path because you want to achieve something amazing rather than live a life of ease and comfort. Yes, you'll do it because once you carry out your mission, then for the rest of your life you've done something significant that can never be taken away. Yes, you'll do it because achieving sustained fulfillment is about passing through and executing the life stages to the utmost of your abilities. Yes, you'll do it because right now the most important thing you can do for yourself and possibly for the world is to create a uniquely personal mission and begin carrying it out. And yes, you'll make this trade because it *must* be done.

## Shooting Stars

Alexander the Great is history's most dramatic example of a shooting star. He burst onto the world stage at 20 years old in 336 BC when his father, King Philip of Macedon, was assassinated. Having been taught by his father to be a fearless warrior and capable general, he was able to take over the command of Philip's army. Within a few years he had conquered all of Greece and the Mediterranean, inspiring his troops by personally leading the cavalry charges. He carried with him a copy of Homer's *Iliad*, and his mission was to surpass Achilles as the greatest warrior of all time. He spent the next 12 years conquering Egypt and Persia, and building the largest empire the world had ever known. Before he could conquer India and the rest of Africa he died suddenly, the victim of either an illness or poisoning, at the age of just 32. Nobody, other than Jesus Christ, has ever made such a big mark on history but died so young.

A few people are able to make a huge impact on the world with their life mission—for better or worse—in a short burst. These are shooting stars, like Jesus and Alexander. But generally, the most lasting and impactful missions are the product of careful management of time and risk over decades. In fact, most of the great missions of history were carried out by individuals who were in relatively good health and lived a long time relative to their contemporaries. For example, Confucius, Mohammed, Catherine the Great, Newton, Gandhi, Mother Theresa, Einstein, Chanel, and Buffett.

Those who carefully pace their work and their mission can go on to accomplish much over a long lifetime. Others allow the mission to consume them. They make a mark while young, but burn out like a shooting star before the full impact of their vision is realized. If you throw everything into yourself as though you are a furnace, you burn out. Seek instead to structure your life as a slow burn. Maintain and rejuvenate your furnace. Manage both your time and your personal energy wisely.

In our modern world there are many examples of shooting stars in the movie and music businesses. Young stars come seemingly out of nowhere and make movies or music that is popular and financially successful. But their careers ultimately crap out. Stars can't keep topping themselves. Sooner or later they will make a movie that earns less at the box office than the previous ones, or they will record music that doesn't sell as well. This does not necessarily mean these stars have stopped being good artists. But frequently it means they are either under external pressure to put out new material before it is ready, or the fruits of their initial successes create distractions.

Nearly everything valuable and meaningful we enjoy in the world today was created by somebody working very hard over a long period of time. Most likely a person who:

- Paradoxically, laid down the basic template of their mission in their twenties or thirties and then pushed it forward relentlessly over the decades, and had "success" in middle age.

- Was very steady and consistent with their work and made no unrecoverable erratic decisions related to their mission or their personal health.

Meryl Streep, with 20 Academy Award nominations and three wins, might be one of the best examples of a "slow burn." She devoted herself to her mission of being a great actor over many decades and has consistently and persistently remained at the top of her game.

Completion of your mission will be the result of continued and consistent work. Success results from repetition. Steady progress toward a deeply personal mission over a sustained period of time is often a key component of true fulfillment. A sudden windfall, reaching an ultimate life goal while still young, or a life of consumption due to early success, can lead to burnout and depression.

## The Mission Track

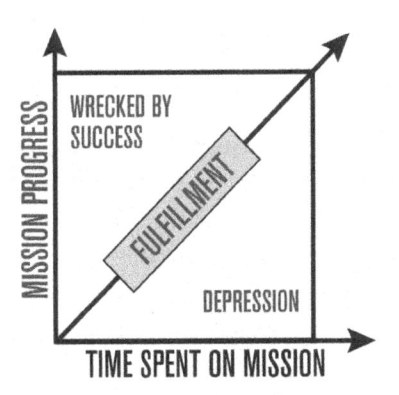

When Julius Caesar saw a statue of Alexander the Great in Spain in 69 BC, he wept. For he realized that by the age of 32 Alexander had conquered the world. But Caesar, who was now the same age, had done nothing for which to be remembered by future generations. By 60 BC, Caesar had rebounded from his despair and was able to win election as one of Rome's consuls. He became the governor of present-day France. Trying to emulate and surpass Alexander and enrich himself, he conquered parts of present-day Germany and Britain. In 50 BC he was ordered by the Senate to disband his army, but he instead marched on Rome and began a civil war. He defeated his enemies and was named Dictator. Over the next few years he increased his own powers significantly while reducing the powers of his opponents. Festivals were held in his honor. Coins bore his likeness. And there were no limits to his authority. In 44 BC a group of senators attacked and assassinated Caesar. They killed him on the senate steps with daggers.

Caesar went from depression to executing an enormous mission to destroying himself through his own successes. Understand as you choose, plan, and execute your mission that *continuous progress along the mission track leads to fulfillment and is the tightrope between depression and being "wrecked by success."*

Lack of fulfillment can lead to depression. And depression can interfere with our ability to live a good life by performing the five life stages well. Depression is a debilitating condition like Caesar experienced when he saw the Alexander statue. It is an emotional state in which a person has feelings of hopelessness and low self-worth, experiences a loss of appetite and energy, and suffers from insomnia and an inability to enjoy life.

At the other extreme, if a person succeeds in their mission too soon or too easily, they can become wrecked by success, a term coined by psychologist Sigmund Freud in 1916. He explained it as a paradox whereby people become neurotic as a result of success. It is as though a person can perform effectively at the highest level and move mountains as long as their objective is in front of them. But as soon as they actually complete their goal, they are unable to handle the white-hot glow of success that ensues from it. The achievement of success can lead to a person feeling unworthy of what they have accomplished and then no longer wanting it. Caesar kept provoking his contemporaries by giving himself new powers and accolades until he essentially forced them to destroy him.

On the mission track a person is alive, alert, and fulfilled due to making continued progress. If a person chooses the wrong mission, too large a mission, or fails to maintain timely progress along their mission track, they can slip into despair and depression. Alternatively, if a person chooses a mission that is too small or they achieve the milestones along the mission track too easily or too early, they can end up unable to handle the intensity of their accomplishments and can be wrecked by success.

Carefully choose a mission track that always challenges you, but is neither too ambitious nor too easy to achieve. When you have setbacks ensure that you do not slip into despair. Always know that whatever problems you face have solutions. When you have victories, maintain your equilibrium. Remember that you deserve your successes, but that the power you wield must be used for constructive ends and to benefit others.

## Beyond the Mission

"I felt something hit me in the right shoulder. A shoe," wrote Steve Madden, the shoe magnate, in his autobiography, *The Cobbler*. Madden's shoe company was going public through a stock offering. He was making a speech to the stock salesmen at Stratton Oakmont, helmed by Jordan Belfort. It was an incident later made famous in the movie, *The Wolf of Wall Street*. "Then I felt another hit my stomach and one at my chest... they truly did not care what I was saying or what I stood for or even what kind of shoes I made. I was just a name on a piece of paper they could sell."

Madden was incredibly driven and effective in executing his mission of building his eponymous shoe company, Steve Madden. He was brilliant both at creating new designs for shoes and as a promoter of his firm. And now, by going public, he had become a multimillionaire. But he wrote: "Relationships were always a big problem in my life...no matter how hard I tried I just couldn't keep a relationship." With no wife or girlfriend or family members to watch his back, Madden fell under the spell of Belfort, one of the most charismatic con men of the 1990s. "Jordan had an air about him that made you sit up straight. Everyone wanted to please him, and I understood right away how he had amassed these disciples."

Through golf junkets via private jet featuring heavy drinking, drugs, and prostitutes, Belfort convinced Madden they were friends. Belfort had Madden flip shares of stock in companies taken public by Stratton Oakmont. As a result, the FBI arrested Madden for fraud, he spent several years in prison, and he nearly lost his company. Madden had achieved business and financial success, fame, the admiration of his celebrity endorsers, and had the world at his feet. But by forming relationships outside of his mission with Belfort and his cadre of swindlers, rather than with people who truly loved him and had his best interests at heart, he was wrecked by his success.

Two decades later, another shoe magnate, Tony Hsieh, faced similar challenges and received a letter from a friend: "I am going to be blunt. I think you are taking too many drugs…. The people you are surrounding yourself with are either ignorant or willing to be complicit in you killing yourself." The letter was written by Grammy Award–winning singer, Jewel. Hsieh's online shoe company, Zappos, had pioneered the business model of encouraging customers to buy as many shoes as they wished and allowed free returns. Zappos was acquired by Amazon for $1.2 billion. According to *Forbes*, Hsieh "experimented with a revolutionary… management philosophy, where no one at Zappos reported to anyone nor carried any titles."

Hsieh's mission was not about shoes, it was about creating a utopian business and then using his fortune to create a utopian community. He acquired nine properties in Park City, Utah, in 2019. Jewel and several of Hsieh's other friends and family members had begun trying to stage interventions as they saw him drinking heavily and making erratic decisions. But in Utah he was able to shut them out and insulate himself among increasingly younger friends. With a net worth of $700 million, "Hsieh retreated to Park City, where he surrounded himself with yes-men," as detailed in *Forbes*. "He would double the amount of their highest-ever salary. All they had to do was move to Park City with him."

Jewel's plea was both prescient and in vain. Hsieh was seriously injured in a fire that many think was related to his heavy nitrous oxide abuse, and he died a few weeks later due to complications from smoke inhalation.

Madden was more fortunate. After serving his time in prison he embraced sobriety and became a husband and father. And with these positive influences in his life, he resumed his mission, diversified his company into apparel, and became a billionaire. He said, "My mistakes, my addiction, my weaknesses, my successes, and my family are all one." We each need a mission to channel our inner essence into a great and fulfilling project, but the bigger we grow it the more we also need to form a family.

# 3. START FAMILY

**Stick Your Neck Out**

Nightclub and casino owner Rick Blaine didn't interfere or lift a finger to help as one of his best customers was arrested and taken away for questioning by the military police. "I stick my neck out for nobody," was all he had to say. The man taken away considered Rick a friend, and the other guests were appalled by this cold-blooded declaration.

As the star of the movie *Casablanca*, Rick is the proprietor of Rick's Café Américain, the most popular watering hole in Morocco during World War II. His "gin joint" has become the place well-to-do war refugees come to try to secure passage to America or Europe. He is a perennially stylishly dressed host in a white dinner jacket, but is a cynical enigma to his patrons. Nothing anyone says impresses Rick, he won't let his customers buy him a drink, and he treats his lover with cold disrespect.

*Casablanca* is considered by many the greatest love story of all time. And the Rick character is perhaps the greatest example of many hardboiled pragmatists played by Humphrey Bogart during Hollywood's golden age. These characters are disillusioned men with great capabilities who appear not to stand for anything but their own self-interest and have no true mission. But sooner or later a chink in this façade inevitably reveals itself.

To exit the young-adult stage and become a true man or woman necessitates a shift in your thinking and values. No longer can you simply concern yourself with your own needs and wants. Now is the time that your biological clock will start ticking louder. And you and many of your contemporaries will start to develop deeper love relationships and consider marriage or other forms of union and starting a family. And to go down that path requires you to place the needs of your loved ones above even yourself. Not because of some calculation about what you and your partner or spouse will do for one another, but because you truly love them and care more about their well-being and needs than you do your own.

An unnamed person called in to the Dennis Prager radio show in December 2021 with regretful words of warning for Prager's audience: "I was married twenty years and I was faithful the first ten. Then I couldn't control myself and I gave in to the temptations that always seemed to be around. The first time it was like the first time shooting someone. I wanted to slit my wrists, because I had a great wife and was racked with guilt. The second and third time I realized, 'This isn't so bad.' After ten years of cheating, my kids convinced my wife to divorce me. Even though I was financially successful and had a lot of sex I missed out on my marriage and being a father. My lack of self-control ate me alive."

What good would it do you to achieve a vibrant mission, enjoy financial success, but betray the people in your life you should care about the most? A real man or woman puts their loved ones above themselves.

Shortly after Rick says he won't stick out his neck, we learn the real reason for his cold exterior. Ilsa, the love of his life, who abandoned Rick in Paris due to a misunderstanding, has come to Casablanca. And accompanying her is husband, Victor Laszlo, a famous freedom fighter and international fugitive. Now we can see that Rick is heartbroken and depressed, and trying to punish the world.

It is a difficult decision. Does Rick help Ilsa and her husband escape to Lisbon so they can lead the resistance against Nazi Germany? Or does he try to win Ilsa back for himself? He takes action. Despite his broken heart, Rick chooses Ilsa's happiness over his own. He shoots a Nazi officer, puts Ilsa and Laszlo on a plane, and flees Morocco, losing his profit-churning club.

Rick has broken his own rule and stuck his neck out, putting somebody else above himself and the pursuit of money. He is no longer dead inside. Rick is a true man. He has left the limbo of Casablanca and can rediscover himself and find his mission. Above all, he can now love again.

## A Complementary Mixture

When they first met at a party, Patrizia Reggiani mesmerized Maurizio Gucci, the heir to the Gucci fortune, with her violet eyes. "For him," wrote Sara Gay Forden in *House of Gucci*, "it was love at first sight; for her, it was the beginning of her conquest of one of Milan's most prominent young bachelors—and one of Italy's most glamorous names." According to Patrizia, people said they were "the most beautiful couple in the world" when they first came together.

There's nothing wrong with being attracted to somebody who is beautiful, famous, or rich. But those qualities are not sufficient in and of themselves to sustain a relationship over the long term. Patrizia ultimately had Maurizio assassinated in a mad quest to obtain his fortune. In a prison-cell interview she was asked why she grew to hate him so much. Was it because he left you? Was it because he began seeing another woman? Patrizia said, "I didn't respect him anymore. He wasn't the man I had married; he didn't have the same ideals anymore." The differences between them had become more accentuated and weren't complementary.

You will sometimes hear people say that opposites attract. But that is a simplification. We tend to partner with people with whom we have much in common, which allows us to relate well to each other. But we also search for a quality in a mate that we lack.

Can you imagine going on a double date with Han Solo and Princess Leia during the early days of their courtship? She wants to go see a space opera, and he wants to slum it at the Star Wars Cantina. She wants to eat caviar and truffles, and he wants to eat bantha burgers with two hands and no napkins. She wants to drink champagne, and he wants to drink whatever's available straight out of the jug until he passes out. They banter constantly, each trying to get the last word, but it is more for fun than a true argument.

Princess Leia and Han Solo were both assertive, outspoken natural leaders. But Leia brought to Han the refined manners and pedigree he lacked. And Han brought to Leia the excitement that comes with willingness to bend the myriad claustrophobic rules she was raised with as a royal. He also was able to protect her in a hostile and dangerous wartime environment. Each was missing something, and each gave the other what they needed.

Japanese novelist Haruki Murakami and his wife Yoko also possess a complementary mixture of skills and traits. "I have no special talent for business, nor am I particularly friendly or social, which makes me ill suited to deal with customers," Murakami wrote of owning a jazz café with Yoko when they were in their twenties. But by working together they were able to overcome each other's shortcomings, pay down their debts, and make the café successful. Now, 40 years later, Murakami has written more than a dozen bestselling novels. He and Yoko still work together; she is his most important writing collaborator.

Yoko is always the first reader Murakami shows his manuscripts to. "She is thus the 'fixed point' in my editing process, the one who knows best how I write." Although Murakami trusts his wife's opinions, "Harsh words are sometimes exchanged. I could never be so direct and honest with an editor—that's the advantage." But ultimately, whether or not he agrees with her comments, Murakami has made it a rule to always rewrite any section Yoko has found fault with. She helps him figure out where the flow of the "reading has been blocked," something he is unable to do for himself.

No person is perfect or complete. Make certain you love the person you intend to marry, but also confirm your similarities and differences are complementary. It will make your relationship stronger and enhance your ability to build a life together. And when the time comes for children, they will benefit if, between the two of you, there is a complementary mixture of attitudes, skills, and capabilities.

## Belong to Someone

"Many have shared in the victories.... But there's only one who has logged as many miles and made as many sacrifices," said Super Bowl champion and two-time NFL MVP Kurt Warner at his Hall of Fame induction ceremony in 2017. "Brenda, I chose you, because of all the people who loved and supported me over the years you, above all others deserved to share this stage with me. The greatest joy in my life has been having you by my side."

When a person wins an Academy Award or is inducted into a sports hall of fame, the person they often thank most emphatically is their spouse. And when a person is elected to a high governmental office, their spouse receives a title too. As soon as Barak Obama was sworn in as America's 44th president in 2009, his wife Michelle became the first lady. This isn't just a matter of titles or symbolism. Amassing the qualifications and connections needed to mount a presidential campaign is incredibly challenging.

And serving as America's head of state and overseeing its governance, economy and military is even more difficult. As a practical matter, few can do these things without a committed and supportive spouse at their side. The American people rightfully refer to presidential wives, who have the extraordinary full-time role of overseeing America's ceremonial events and working to advance social causes, as the first lady. The converse applies as well. Barak Obama ran for election against John McCain, whose running mate for vice president was Sarah Palin, the governor of Alaska. To become a state governor also requires having a committed and supportive spouse. During the election Sarah and the media referred to her husband Todd Palin as Alaska's "first dude." (It should be noted that the actual term for a husband of a female president or governor is "first gentleman.")

In a successful marriage both partners realize how important each is to the other as a source of personal and professional support and as a co-parent. The president and first lady and governor and first dude are excellent examples of how your spouse is the most important person in your life. More important than even your own parents or your children.

There's no way to really understand what marriage—a lifetime personal and financial commitment that often produces new human beings—is like without actually going through it. But here are some of the primary reasons why happily married people cherish their spouses:

- *Confide.* It is critical to one's well-being to be able to confide in your spouse and receive their input as a sounding board when you are confused or things aren't going well. Even your mom, best friend, or platonic roommate can't help you in this area as well as someone with whom you live and share every aspect of your life.

- *Belong.* It is reassuring and satisfying to "belong" to someone who you can trust to get their share of things done, be it making money, taking care of the house and kids, planning vacations and social events, or caring for one another when ill. This is what is meant when people speak about spouses being partners.

- *Love.* Dating, and the fun and lust that comes with it, is intoxicating, but it isn't truly love. In order to truly love another person, you have to accumulate years of experiences when you were each real and vulnerable to each other. Marriage is the primary vehicle, other than being a parent, that allows this accumulation to occur.

There's a difference between being in a casual relationship with someone and being in an accountable relationship like a marriage or civil union. When you agree to spend your lives together you become accountable to one another, because your decisions in almost every area of life will affect each other. You want to marry a spouse who, like Brenda said of Kurt Warner, is "the best partner, best friend, best parent, and best person I've ever known."

## Ultimately, We're Builders

"Open it! Open it or I will!" Betty shouted at her husband, Don, in the critically acclaimed drama *Mad Men*. His shoulders slumped in defeat. Out of the locked desk drawer came a battered shoebox. In it were yellowed photos inscribed with captions. All evidence that "Don Draper" was an alias. The man to whom Betty thought she had been married for ten years was really named Dick Whitman and had another wife and another family. Everything she thought she had built with this wealthy, handsome Madison Avenue advertising executive was as much a lie as the advertising slogans he effortlessly churned out for his clients.

"I can explain," his fingers twitched and he dropped his cigarette. "Yes, I'm sure you can," Betty replied, "you are a very talented storyteller."

Betty and Don are the quintessential example of a couple who, from the outside, look like they have it all. They are beautiful, impeccably dressed, have two cute kids, and a giant house in the suburbs. However, in actuality they've built nothing together. Don has concocted a false persona of the perfect 1950s man, under a name that isn't even his, and which is an oppressive weight that causes him to drink heavily and constantly cheat on Betty. And Betty, a former fashion model, cares only about trying to preserve her beauty as she ages and as the world's changing values slowly pull the rug out from under her feet.

How could Don and Betty have anything meaningful to say to each other or build anything together when their entire marriage is based on twin facades and each has no idea who the other really is? How could they possibly build a strong marriage that would allow them to succeed together?

As you go into your marriage, always try to keep in mind that:

- *Spending time with your partner should feel comfortable and natural.* If, like the Drapers, you can't have an easily flowing conversation, that should be a red flag. Conversation should come easily because you and your partner are interested in similar things and share common viewpoints and values.

- *Marriage isn't perfect, but it is whatever you build it into day after day.* It grows through all the little daily details: cooking dinner when you're tired, having conversations, and taking out the trash. Even if you are as fantastic-looking as the Drapers, every marriage requires daily ongoing work in order to flourish.

- *You need connections to the world outside your mission.* When you're young you can and should lose yourself in adventures and your mission. Go all in. Commit fully. But as you grow older you need relationships with people you love in the external world too. Don had only this work mission to live for, and everything else was a cover story and a fabrication. If you have a spouse, you have both a mission and someone with whom to share your mission.

Ultimately you are builders. You are working together to build a life, a home, and a family. When tensions arise, try reminding each other you chose to pool your resources together to build something great. Try to stay in equilibrium with one another, because marriage is a long haul. And remember, pursuing private goals in parallel will not lead to shared success.

"We exchanged audiences," said Jay-Z of his marriage to Beyoncé. She helped his "Bonnie & Clyde" track go to number one. "What I gave her was a street credibility, a different edge." Many in the music industry consider the union a marriage and a merger. The "president and first lady of the music industry" grossed $250 million with their *On the Run II* tour in 2018.

That is the secret to any marriage partners succeeding together. You have to be able to apply your combined skills toward objectives you both share, and you have to want to be successful for each other.

## Your In-Laws

"All right now look, Focker, I'm a patient man. That's what 19 months in a Vietnamese prison camp will do to you," Jack said, pointing two fingers at his own eyes and then jabbing them in the direction of his son-in-law-to-be, Greg Focker. "And if I find out that you are trying to corrupt my first-born child I will bring you down, baby!" says Jack Byrnes in the comedy *Meet the Parents*. We learn it is very difficult for any newcomer to stay inside Jack's "circle of trust."

*You always marry the family*, as the saying goes. Your spouse's family will likely have a significant amount of influence over a number of decisions that will affect you. And that leads to a variety of factors that make your relationships with your in-laws very different from the other relationships in your life—and often very tricky.

There was a couple, Peter and Alexis, who were talking about how to spend the upcoming summer vacation. "When we go with your family, it's always to that same dude ranch every year," Peter said, "and your mom plans the same activities for us every time. Then your dad tells the same jokes at dinner every night." Alexis frowned, "Yes, but that's relaxing for me. My mom and my sisters help with the kids. But when we travel with your family it's always in some country with no paved roads or clean water, and nobody speaks English, and it's not safe."

Keep in mind that having complementary traits is one reason you married each other. It is possible that a "missing ingredient" that attracted your spouse to you could be intimidating or off-putting to your in-laws. Where your in-laws are concerned, your goals should be:

- First and foremost, *never do anything or say anything to your in-*

*laws that would cause embarrassment or pain to your spouse.* Do everything you can to avoid having any lingering tension or awkwardness when you spend time around your in-laws.

- Interact with your in-laws *as a single unit with your spouse.* Don't contradict one another or allow your in-laws to try to ferret out your opinions separately from the two of you. Either support your spouse's stance or say, "Sweetie, can we talk about that later?"

- Any time your in-laws do something you don't like, *remind yourself, that it's nothing personal.* It really isn't. If you're going to err on the side of being patient, flexible, understanding and giving the benefit of the doubt to anyone in your life, make certain it is your in-laws.

- Set limits on what you allow your in-laws to say or do when it comes to your marriage, home, and kids. Through your spouse they probably know more about you than anyone but your own family. However, *they are in a relationship with your spouse, not with you.* They're not a third partner in your marriage.

- If you feel you are losing your patience with your in-laws, remind yourself *they knew and nurtured your spouse for many years before you came along.* The relationship they formed with your spouse is precious to them, and you do not have the right to intrude upon it.

Don't try to be the perfect son-in-law or daughter-in-law, because that is very difficult to do. And don't expect your spouse's parents to be the perfect in-laws to you either. Be patient with each other. And know that eventually grandchildren will likely make the relationship infinitely easier by providing a focal point for conversations and activities.

"When you marry, your spouse has a past and their family does too," wrote Paul Theroux in *Hotel Honolulu*. "You are attaching yourself to that past. What they did or didn't do affects you in the present. So you should know their histories. And you should share your history with your spouse."

## The Most Delightful People

"It gets a whole lot more complicated when you have kids," said Bob, a famous American actor making a commercial in Japan, trying to reassure young newlywed Charlotte in the film *Lost in Translation*, "Your life as you know it is gone. Never to return. But they learn how to walk and they learn how to talk. And you want to be with them. And they turn out to be the most delightful people you'll ever meet in your life."

When you become a parent for the first time, you are no longer the tip of a branch or a dead-end on somebody else's family line. Now you have established your own family tree. You've created a new life and a new bloodline. And what new parents quickly come to realize is that being a parent isn't just a new role, like being a homeowner, or a new set of obligations, like adopting a puppy. It is a completely new *lifestyle*. At all times now, and every time you make any decision, you always have to ask yourself *What's best for my child?*

What is best for your child, even before they are old enough to understand it, includes making sure they always feel that they are your priority. They need to feel love from you, and they need to receive time and attention from you. Feed your child. Bathe your child. Hold them when they are cold or when they need to feel another person's touch. These are the most important "chores" you'll ever do! Enjoy the choice you are making to treat this new life as your highest priority.

This is how you show them they are valuable. And they need to feel valuable in order to become happy children and to eventually become well-adjusted adults. We find a way to carve out time for the things that truly matter to us. To be a great parent does not require a lot of money or a lot of education or a high IQ. It requires dedication.

"I was having the emotions of a man who felt that he should be taking care of his family," wrote John Fogerty, the Grammy Award–winning lead singer of Credence Clearwater Revival, about recurring nightmares he experienced while in Denmark pursuing his music career away from his young kids. So he went back, but it was too late. "I had ruined it. The truth is you can never go back…. I have three wonderful children…. But I was a terrible father—terrible. Just inept. It's a shame for the kids, because they had a dad who was loving but wasn't very nurturing in the sense of realizing what my role was. I was not a very involved dad. I was just sort of existing."

Even after a short time of serving as a parent, it can become difficult to remember what life was like before having a small child completely dependent on you. *Did I really have that much free time? Why did I think all that vacationing and eating out was so alluring? I wouldn't trade it for this.* They need you, every single day. So go ahead and enjoy your baby. Enjoy being a parent and the process of building your family.

If you are unable, or can't afford, or don't want to have children, that in no way limits you from participating in the family stage of life or pursuing the fulfillment that comes with it. Be an aunt or an uncle. Be a teacher. Be a coach. Be a mentor. And carefully read and consider the *Extra Parents* section that comes later in this book. It describes how we are all likely to be needed as parents at some point, whether we have our own biological children or not.

And though Charlotte in *Lost in Translation* is a young adult rather than a kid, middle-aged Bob essentially acts as an empathetic "extra parent" for her as well. Although he is a busy actor, he still makes time to reassure her without being preachy or talking down. Life, including marriage and parenthood, is hard, but it contains unlimited possibilities. When Charlotte asked him what he was doing here in Japan, Bob replied in jest, "Taking a break from my wife. Forgetting my son's birthday. And, uh, getting paid two million dollars to endorse whiskey when I could be doing a play somewhere."

## A Project with Your Kids

Tom Brady's dad would try to come home from work early enough in the afternoons to hit baseballs to him at a nearby field. Tom grew up going to watch San Francisco 49ers football games, but his father, Tom Senior, didn't push him to be a football player. Tom Senior had helped Tom's three older sisters become standout high school and college softball players. Tom grew up attending their softball games, and his goal was to become a Major League Baseball player.

In high school, Brady wasn't planning to play football, but his school's quarterback was injured, so he decided to give it a try. He did well. His dad wanted him to play college football at nearby Cal-Berkeley, but Brady decided to accept a scholarship to play at Michigan instead. He played professional football for twenty-three years and holds the record for most Super Bowls played (10) and most Super Bowls won (seven). Brady said, "My dad is my best friend. No son could have had a better father."

When Andre Agassi was five years old, his father decided his son was going to be a professional tennis player. Mike Agassi, Andre's father, was a former Olympic boxer who had emigrated to Las Vegas from Iran. He required Agassi to hit 2,500 tennis balls a day beginning at the age of seven years old, which works out to almost one million per year.

When he was thirteen Andre's dad decided his son would never be able to play tennis professionally if he didn't start training full time. So he had Andre move to Florida by himself where he trained and lived at the Bollettieri Tennis Academy, skipped college, and went pro. He played professional tennis for twenty years and is one of only four players to have won all four Grand Slam tournaments. "I play tennis for a living even though I hate tennis," Andre said at one point, "My dad chose my life for me."

Childhood is mainly a period of preparation, so approach parenting as though you are working on a project with each of your kids. That project is the preparation to live a fulfilling life. Focus on helping your child become a responsible person with good character who has good academic and social skills. That will prepare them for the adult life stages and allow them to succeed at whatever they choose to do. It isn't your right or your duty as a parent to attempt to choose your child's occupation or calling for them.

Parenting is "a project with your kids":

- *Be willing to put in a lot of time and effort to help them become who they are going to become.* Be both present and available every day to influence your kids. It is your responsibility—not their teachers', coaches', friends' or social media's—to be the biggest influence in their lives.

- *Expect a lot of ups and downs.* They're kids, so you can't expect them to make continuous steady daily progress on anything. Even if your child is a tennis prodigy, don't ask them to do the same massive workout every single day. Do they need to be pushed today, or do they need a day off? Tailor what you teach.

- *Children learn more from example than through lectures.* Make certain you teach them responsibility, discipline, and respect for others through your actions. And show that you trust them by giving them chores and tasks and holding them responsible for completing them. Let them make a great many of their own choices.

Early adulthood is all about pouring energy into yourself and your mission. In later life spending time with your spouse and kids becomes very important too. Among the most fulfilling experiences a parent can have is taking your kid to their first day of school or their sports tryout knowing they are ready and can handle themself. You did your job. You prepared them.

## I'm Proud of You

There was a high school basketball player, with an ankle-to-thigh plaster cast, named Tanya. She put her crutches into the back of her mother's car and maneuvered herself into the passenger seat. Tanya's basketball team had an important game tonight and she wouldn't be able to play due to her injury.

Tanya's mom knew how disappointed her daughter was about this season-ending injury, so she didn't try to make conversation during the car ride. She allowed Tanya to be alone with her thoughts. She knew Tanya felt it was important to be with the team even if she couldn't play, particularly since she was their captain. And she knew it made Tanya sad to watch her teammates play without her.

They were both still getting used to how long it took to move around with the crutches, and they barely made it into the gym as the game was starting. Her teammates on the bench were excited to see Tanya and she started moving toward them.

Then Tanya's mom saw her move to the left of the bench and keep going, and she wasn't sure why. Was Tanya too sad to sit with her friends? She watched as Tanya swung her body around with her crutches, and sat next to a smaller girl who was sitting by herself. Tanya started chattering away. Then her mother understood. One of Tanya's teammates had a younger sister, Sally, with special needs. Apparently, Tanya had perceived that Sally was alone at the game and had decided to keep her company.

Tanya's team eked out a win, even without her. And she took Sally with her to go and congratulate the team. Sally's dad came running over and thanked Tanya and said something about having had to step out for some kind of emergency. Sally gave Tanya a hug and went with her dad. As they walked out into the cold night air, Tanya's mom was choked up and her eyes were watery as she whispered, "I've seen you do a lot of amazing things in that gym, but I've never been more proud of you than I am right now."

Your kids need to hear "I'm proud of you" as often as possible. "I love you" is also important, but it is unconditional. We love our kids just for being exactly as they are. "I'm proud of you" let's them know they are on the right track with their behavior and actions. Deep down this is what every child, and every person no matter their age, craves from their parents.

We all want our children to excel, but even more importantly, we want them to be good people. For that to happen we need to teach and motivate them every day. If we try to motivate them with yelling and lectures and punishments it won't work in the long term. Praise and constructive feedback that helps our children develop pride in who they are works much better.

Yes, there are going to be times that you will have to use strong words to help your child stay on track, but try to at least make it a 3:1 ratio of positive reinforcement to criticism. People instinctively do that even with their pets—three pats on the head for every "No!"

When your kid struggles it can be frustrating and embarrassing for them and for you. But you can't let it show to them or to anyone. You have to be a rock for them. More often than not these situations only *seem* to go on forever. In hindsight they were temporary and were short in duration. And there will be more in the years ahead.

When your kid faces a setback help them find a way to overcome the adversity, but let them solve their own problem rather than handling it for them. Provide them a stable world within which to have victories and losses. Remind them every day that you love them, they are valuable, and they matter. When they are suffering tell them, "Everything's going to be all right," and when they do well, be sure to tell them, "I'm proud of you."

## Extra Parents

Oprah Winfrey "was dubbed 'The Preacher' for her uncanny ability to memorize Bible verses" and recite them at the local church. Her maternal grandmother, Hattie Mae, raised Oprah for the first six years of her life in Mississippi while her mother traveled and searched for work. Hattie Mae was very poor. She made potato-sack dresses for Oprah, taught her to read before she turned three, and instilled deep religious faith in her granddaughter.

No matter how great a set of parents any child is blessed with, every kid gets too much of some things and not enough of other things from their "primary parents." That can make a child unbalanced and off-kilter in some areas. They need coaches, teachers, bosses, godparents, uncles, aunts, neighbors, and family friends to help fill in and smooth out what they've learned from their primary parents. In fact, all children need "extra parents."

An excellent example of this concept is provided by the book, *Rich Dad, Poor Dad*, by Robert Kiyosaki, which has sold over 35 million copies. "I had two fathers, a rich one and a poor one," Kiyosaki wrote, "Both earned substantial incomes. Yet one always struggled financially. The other would become one of the richest men in Hawaii."

The book describes how Kiyosaki's biological father was a Stanford-educated PhD who followed traditional career thinking and always had difficulty making ends meet. His "extra father" was his best friend's dad, a high school dropout who followed an entrepreneurial path, employed thousands of people, and left tens of millions of dollars to charities. For Kiyosaki, who had significant business and philanthropic ambitions, having an extra parent who could counsel him on topics his primary parents could not drastically altered the trajectory of his life.

One of the most dramatic illustrations of an extra parent is that provided by Mr. Miyagi, who serves as Daniel Larusso's martial arts instructor in the movie *The Karate Kid*. Poor Daniel has just moved to California from New Jersey with his mom, and is continually being pummeled by a group of high school bullies who train in karate. Mr. Miyagi, a Japanese handyman who also happens to be a karate black belt, takes Daniel under his wing. He does a wonderful job of helping Daniel in three areas every child needs extra parents:

- *Setting an example of how to behave.* Mr. Miyagi brings Daniel to the bullies' hulking karate instructor, Sensei Kreese. He suggests the boys settle this matter via a karate showdown at a tournament. He remains calm and polite while Kreese treats him with insolence.

- *Providing supplemental ethical instruction.* Before teaching Daniel karate, Mr. Miyagi requires him to do many hours of manual labor. Daniel is taught to "eat your peas before your dessert." He is also taught that to enter the karate world he must first provide an offering. These are character lessons he isn't learning at home.

- *Teaching skills at an expert level.* All that hard labor Daniel did for Mr. Miyagi was disguised conditioning and muscle-memory training. From this foundation, Mr. Miyagi rapidly teaches Daniel karate. He defeats his nemesis, Johnny, and is crowned a karate champion.

If you are a coach, teacher, uncle, aunt, or family friend trying to help in a child's development, take a close look at Mr. Miyagi's example. He was firm at times with Daniel, but never harsh. Mr. Miyagi did not see it as his role to discipline Daniel or try to be his father. Rather, he was a guide and a confidant. He sought to enhance and add to what Daniel was taught by his mother, not challenge or disregard her teachings. He set a tone of learning through mutual enjoyment of their time together. Miyagi showed Daniel by example how to behave like a person of character and as an adult.

## Warts and Imperfections

"Some guys think the most important thing in their life is their job, the stock market, whatever. To me it was my kids. The question I asked myself was, how well could a kid develop if you provided him with the perfect environment?" said Marv Marinovich. He had played football for USC, and the Oakland Raiders hired him in the 1970s as the NFL's first strength and conditioning coach. He wanted to develop the perfect quarterback and started by marrying the sister of a USC star quarterback. While she was pregnant, he kept her on a stringent diet. When their son, Todd, was born he was fed only fresh vegetables, fruit, and raw milk. Marv started him on a physical conditioning program when he was only a month old. Todd went his entire childhood without eating any food that contained refined sugar or white flour. From the time he was old enough to play organized football, Marv always had him play with and against older kids.

In high school Todd broke the Orange County record for passing yards. In 1988 he appeared on the cover of *California* magazine with the headline, "The Making of a Perfect Athlete," and *Sports Illustrated* published an article discussing his father's desire to turn his son into the "perfect quarterback." He became the first freshman quarterback to start the first game of the season for USC since World War II, and he went on to lead the team to a Rose Bowl victory that year.

The following year his play became erratic. He was benched for skipping classes and arrested for cocaine possession. Despite these setbacks, Todd was still drafted by the Raiders, but had serious substance-abuse issues throughout his short NFL career. He routinely used a teammate's urine to pass his drug tests, and the Raiders staged an intervention and forced him to go into rehabilitation. He left the league shortly thereafter and spiraled into even worse drug abuse. It was later revealed that even during his high school years he had been a heavy drug user in order to cope with the pressures of his unorthodox upbringing.

You are under no obligation to try to give your kids a perfect life, nor are your kids under any obligation to try to be perfect for you.

- It is admirable to want the best for your children and to have high expectations. But *your expectations need to be reasonable*. It isn't reasonable to expect your kids to be perfect at anything.

- Even going back in time to the dawn of man, there has never been a perfect parent. *There has never been a perfect child*. And no person has ever had a perfect childhood.

- *The more perfect a parent tries to make their child's life*, the less happy they will be once they grow up. It would be a disservice to raise an adult who believes their life is supposed to be perfect.

- In order to learn how to ski, you have to fall a lot. To learn to do anything well requires a lot of trial and error. You will make many mistakes as a parent, and *your child will make a lot of mistakes as they learn*. Achievers are imperfect and make mistakes.

- The best gift you can give your child isn't a perfect life. The best gift is to *teach them how to live a life of good character* and ensure they receive a good education.

When your first child is born everyone tends to think they are going to become president of the United States or an NFL quarterback. Eventually you get to the point where some windows have closed, and it becomes a bit of a relief to lovingly point out their shortcomings: "Well, with a raspy voice like that I guess he's never going to become a backup singer for Lady Gaga."

Don't wish for perfect children. Enjoy them with all their warts and imperfections. Love them just as they are. Recognize that to become a great and fulfilled adult doesn't require starting off as a perfect kid.

## Can You Teach?

"The stench in the cellar came from herrings that were stored there, twenty barrels of them," wrote G. I. Gurdjieff in his mystical tome, *Meetings with Remarkable Men*. He took a quick look at some iron beds he wished to purchase and then fled the cellar. Out on the street he began negotiations with the owner, an army provisions contractor. The contractor told Gurdjieff he was livid that he had paid for 20 barrels of rotten herrings and now also had to incur the expense of hauling them to the dump.

Gurdjieff was a Greek-Armenian "master" in the early 1900s. A master is one who can teach others and create the conditions under which they can quest for knowledge. He was on a mission, which encompassed extensive journeys to unlock the mysteries of "pre-sand Egypt." Falling back on his teachings, Gurdjieff quickly assessed the situation. Rotten fish was an excellent fertilizer. So he could probably arrange for a gardener to remove the barrels for no charge, clean the barrels, and deliver them to his workshop. Barrels were in short supply, so Gurdjieff could sell them for a premium. He told the army contractor he would remove the herring barrels in exchange for an additional discount on the iron beds. The contractor gladly agreed.

Gurdjieff praises his many teachers in *Remarkable Men*: mystics, priests, and princes. But the one he placed above all others was his father. Gurdjieff describes how he was able to easily master any new skill he needed, or easily raise funds whenever necessary, as his mission to acquire lost ancient knowledge took him around the world. This was because of the way his father taught him as a child in the late 1800s: "His aim was not that I should learn all sorts of crafts but should develop in myself the ability to surmount the difficulties presented by any new kind of work." His father taught him to see situations in their entirety, not to profit from the misfortunes of others, and to solve problems in ways that would benefit all. Owing to this education and set of teachings, Gurdjieff could make or repair almost any item with his hands, and make money at will with his mind.

A hundred years ago, in Gurdjieff's time, nearly every parent expected to have to teach their children basic skills like how to repair broken items, cook meals, clean the home, launder and mend clothing, do basic carpentry, and build a fire. In today's world kids don't have as many chores as they once did, and there is more outsourcing of manual tasks. Also, there is much more of an expectation on the part of parents that school teachers, coaches, private instructors, tutors, and camps will teach children the skills they need to succeed in life. Parents are more responsible for arranging and paying for instruction and providing transportation for their kids. But if parents don't put in the work to teach their kids basic tasks like those listed above, how will they be able to teach them broader and more significant life tasks like:

- Treating people respectfully
- Managing their time
- Negotiating with contractors
- Handling personal finances
- Interviewing for jobs
- Helping those in need

Can you teach? Like Gurdjieff's father, seek through your teaching to show your kids how to solve problems. Rather than teaching one-off formulas, try to explain an overall method and thought process that can be adapted to tackle many types of problems and challenges.

Gurdjieff brought one of the barrels back to his workshop so he could show the value of the herrings as fertilizer. When he opened the barrel and his gardener friend smelled the pungent herrings, he exclaimed, "Now that's what I call herrings!" Gurdjieff was able to pay the gardener to help him sell all the herrings to other herring connoisseurs for an even greater profit than they would have fetched as fertilizer. He then took the army provisions contractor to dinner, explained what happened and offered to split the profits. Everyone benefited from the principles and mindset Gurdjieff's father had taught him. Be a mom or a dad, but also be a teacher.

## Everything Is Amplified

*Damn it, son, my 100-year-old grandmother can run faster than you! Let's move!* This is something one of the great stock characters from the movies, the drill sergeant, might say. He is loud, brash, bombastic, and always overbearing. There's Sergeant Foley in *An Officer and a Gentleman,* Sergeant Hartman in *Full Metal Jacket,* and Sergeant Hulka in *Stripes.* Even outer space has Sergeant Apone in *Alien.*

He is a movie caricature rather than a real military man, so he's a little psychotic. The only way he is able to communicate is by positioning his face an inch away from yours and screaming as loud as he can. He is constantly making up demeaning nicknames for you, inspecting your footlocker for jelly donuts, and demanding to know, "What is your major malfunction?" But at the end of the day, his sole objective is to push you hard so he can indoctrinate and train you with the toughest love possible.

As a parent, you are not trying to be anyone's drill sergeant. But when you get, shall we say, *enthusiastic* with your parenting, can you imagine how you might appear to your child? You are physically bigger and truly a larger-than-life authority figure, like every good movie sergeant only wishes in his wildest dreams he could be.

Try to keep this in mind with your parenting style. Everything you do is bigger and more amplified from the perspective of your kids. Sometimes, even a small scolding about some trivial matter can be debilitating to your children, while a small act of encouragement can help them climb mountains.

On one hand, you don't want to spoon-feed your kids the answer sheet to life's challenges. But on the other hand, you don't want to ram your teachings and worldview down their throats. Do your best to guide your children rather than inadvertently smothering them.

- *Drill sergeants dominate.* As a parent, find a tone for speaking with your child that is neutral and contains no threat of any kind. Neither patronize nor try to have the implicit upper hand. Listen, communicate, and repeat. Distinguish between what they think they want and what they actually need. Establish true rapport.

- *Drill sergeants over-instruct.* As a parent you have to give your kids stern instruction about a few things that could otherwise be devastating or catastrophic. "Don't play with matches," and "look both ways before you cross the street," for example. But your children will tune you out if you try to warn them of every one of life's minor pitfalls. Let them discover some things for themselves.

- *Drill sergeants hunt for mistakes.* As a parent it is better to create a desire for improvement in your kids than an anxiety of being called out for making mistakes. Allow your children to grow by trying difficult things and having some setbacks and failures. Be available to help with encouragement and suggestions.

A drill sergeant's objective is to indoctrinate his people for the very important task of being able to fight together in a war. You are a peacetime parent! In ancient times war between competing tribes was a constant and children weren't viewed as independent human beings. They were considered the property of their parents, and parents had absolute power over them. Every child was expected to enter the same trade as their parents or work in the family business, and to fight for the tribe. Those times are over.

Don't try to train and drill your children into replicas of yourself. The last thing you want is for your kid to end up being your clone or your "Mini Me." Allow them to go beyond you and develop their own unique persona and style. Teach them to have an imagination and show them how to set goals. True success will be to ultimately be able to say, "They're better than we ever were."

## Born Unempathetic

"Unless you stop loafing and trading on your handsome face to fool gullible little girls, and come into your manhood, there is nothing before you but bankruptcy and ruin," said Ernest Hemingway's mother as she threw him out of the house. Hemingway grew up in an affluent household and was pampered during his early life. Fortunately, it wasn't too late for his mother to discipline him. He went on to win a Nobel Prize and become one of the world's greatest writers, introducing a new style of simple prose and economy of words.

The worst curse you can lay on any child's head is to reward them too often and discipline them too little. Spoiled children grow up to become unproductive adults who can't function as friends, spouses, or employees. Show love for your kids by setting clear rules and limits and by disciplining them when necessary.

- *Born Unempathetic.* Nobody is born a "bad" person. Rather, babies are born without empathy. It is up to parents to teach their children how to walk a mile in someone else's shoes and understand the feelings of others at as young an age as possible. The older your kids become without developing empathy, the more difficult it will be to teach, and it may not be possible beyond a certain age.

- *Set limits and rules.* Being flexible with your children is great, but giving them freedom with no explicit limits is not a good idea. No matter how far out you set limits, your kids will want to test them. It is better to start with firm guidelines and relax them over time than to start with overly loose rules and then try to rein them in.

- *Developing willpower.* We aren't born with willpower. It has to be developed over time. You have to teach your kids through rules, positive feedback, and occasional discipline how to develop self-control and to delay gratification. This comes from showing them how to make a daily plan to allocate mandatory tasks, such as chores and homework, in a reasonable ratio to activities they want to do, such as playing with friends and eating snacks.

- *It's not "our" wealth.* Don't get "wrecked by success." And more importantly, don't let your children get wrecked by *your* success. Whatever level of wealth and possessions you have accumulated through your hard work, make certain your kids know these resources belong to you and your spouse, not to the family at large. You are sharing with them only until they can produce their own.

- *I'm disappointed.* When you do have to discipline your children, try to emphasize that you are disappointed with their actions rather than angry at them. You are not disciplining your children as a form of revenge punishment, but rather are acting logically and objectively with a goal of helping them make progress.

As William Deresiewicz points out in *Excellent Sheep*, an overindulgent parent—"the kind who lets their kids run wild in restaurants"—is engaging in a form of overprotection and infantilization. Parents who unleash their children on the world without having taught them good manners and how to behave are being unfair to their kids. And they are showing disrespect to other people in the world—teachers, coaches, neighbors, aunts, uncles, bosses—who are then forced to do the parents' job for them.

Hemingway's mother put many demands on him during his teen years in an effort to direct his adolescent energy. After achieving fame as a novelist, Hemingway was asked in an interview what is the best early training for being a writer. He gave a tongue-in-cheek answer that was probably a backhanded compliment to his mother: "An unhappy childhood."

## The Family Glue

The room is dark and covered in expensive wood paneling, and a silver-haired man with a jutting jaw and the weight of the world on his shoulders sits behind a desk. Marlon Brando is at his smoldering best as Vito Corleone at the beginning of the 1972 film, *The Godfather*. It is one of a series of scenes that take place at the wedding of Corleone's only daughter at his sprawling Long Island estate. And we see all the clues laid before us that this is a powerful man who is obsessed with traditions.

Family is everything to Corleone, the godfather. And although he is hosting a party, he doesn't seem to be celebrating. For the godfather it is a day of meeting obligations and honoring traditions rather than an opportunity for partying. One of the traditions he must follow is that on this wedding day, anyone may come to his study and make a request of him, either small or large.

Corleone is an Italian-American immigrant. And this identity is reflected in the traditions we see on display. Italian food and music, a Catholic wedding reception, and the godfather receiving special visitors privately while garbed in his tuxedo.

Family traditions like these are the glue that hold a family together through the generations. They serve as a foundation and are the backbone underlying a family's strength and cohesiveness. Traditions like these are a constant through the years that bring family members back together and renew the family itself. It is your obligation as a parent to continue or create traditions for your family that help you remember who you are and that rejuvenate the members of the family when they come together.

- *Mark every milestone.* One of the basics of family traditions is that special occasions like holidays, births, birthdays, graduations, weddings, and funerals must be commemorated. People are always busy living their lives, but you are never too busy to make time for the family and mark important milestones. At one wedding you'll be a ring bearer, at another you'll be a groom, and eventually you may be the godfather. Participating in milestones through the years makes the family a living organism.

- *Daily customs.* "Never forget, you're a Vermeil," is what Dick Vermeil, the future NFL Super Bowl winning coach, was told by his dad every single time he walked out the front door during his childhood. These types of daily customs are another building block of tradition. The family belongs to each of its members. And all the members, no matter how young, are responsible for maintaining the family's good name and reputation.

- *Do you have traditions?* One family in your area might be known as musicians; it has concert violinist parents and kids who formed a rock band. Another family has that huge house on the corner where everyone has a standing invitation to hang out anytime. Does your family have its own internal traditions, and is it known to the external world for having its own unique identity? If not, then what is going to hold your family together over time?

In the Introduction to the 50th anniversary version of the novel *The Godfather* by Mario Puzo, the author's son wrote: "The Don, strangely enough, was based on my grandmother. Whenever the Don opened his mouth, my father said that in his own mind he heard the voice of his mother."

As you grew up your parents programmed you with their explicit teachings and also implicitly via the family traditions in which they immersed you. Now you must do the same for the next generation. You've done the best you could with your innate talents and the investment of time and love you received from your parents. Now it is your turn to pass down these traditions to your children and find ways to expand and improve upon them.

## Your Kids Aren't Your Mission

"After years of insomnia and anxiety, I embarked on an odyssey," said famous surfer, Dorian "Doc" Paskowitz, of stepping away from his successful medical practice in Hawaii. As the trailer for the movie *Surfwise* says, Doc decided to "give it all up and spend the rest of his life traveling with his family in a tiny camper from one wave to another."

Throughout the 1970s, Doc, his wife, Juliet, and their nine kids lived in a 24-foot camper pursuing a bohemian lifestyle along the coastlines of California, Baja, Texas, Louisiana, Florida and New England. Doc wanted to spend as much time as he could with his children, and made them his mission. They traveled from one surf break to another, and their lives revolved around surfing, fitness, eating natural food, and being educated in a number of eclectic topics rather than a traditional school curriculum.

The Paskowitz kids became champion surfers. But eventually, as they entered their teenage years, they began to rebel. Due to their nomadic lifestyle, the kids were not able to form enduring relationships with people from outside the family. They also had little privacy, lived in extreme poverty, had to share everything including clothing, and most of their paper records and photos were destroyed by the rigors of their constant travel.

In the end, Doc's attempt at self-fulfillment and a utopian lifestyle backfired. He was pursuing adventures that he probably should have undertaken before having a family. The Paskowitz kids left the never-ending road trip when they became adults, and many of them were estranged from Doc. They blamed him for their lack of life skills and formal education, which prevented them from earning a living and functioning in society. "We weren't trained to do anything but surf," said Doc's son Izzy Paskowitz.

A person must never let their children become their mission. There is a time and place within a person's life for both mission and children, but for the good of each they must be kept separate.

- *Newborns need constant care and attention.* For a period of time parents may have to make their infant children their highest priority.

- *Providing for children is expensive.* For a period of time one or both parents may have to make career and earning income their highest priority.

- *As children grow out of infancy their parents will regain the flexibility to put more time and effort into their missions.* It is important to establish a mission before becoming a parent so as not to think your kids are your mission, like Doc did.

- *Don't live vicariously through your kids.* Treating your child as your mission puts a lot of pressure on them and your relationship with them.

Making your kids your mission usually ends badly, because as adults they often pull away and blame the parent for any misfortune. And the parent finds themselves adrift with no meaning in their life or viable path to fulfillment. "I always thought that career comes first," said Oscar-winning actor Morgan Freeman in a 2016 interview with *Esquire*. "Family is a support mechanism. It doesn't work the other way around."

As a parent you don't want to feel you sacrificed everything, yet have a strained relationship with your kids, like Doc Paskowitz, Marv Marinovich, or Mike Agassi did. On your deathbed, "I was a great parent" won't be enough. You need other forms of mission and legacy too. But "I was a bad parent" will tarnish your other accomplishments. Keep your mission and your children separate or you risk not doing a good job with either.

## I Can't Stop You

"I see what you're up to. It's not the life I would have chosen for you, but it's not my decision. And you know what? I'm okay with it. It's got nothing to do with me. I couldn't stop you if I wanted to, could I?"

These words from a father speaking to his adult son, played by Ray Liotta and Johnny Depp, create an incredibly real and sad and believable moment in the biographical movie *Blow* about the dark underbelly of cocaine in the 1980s. The backdrop for the scene is a spectacular mansion and sports-car collection owned by the son. The father knows in his gut that something isn't quite right, but he also knows his son is now an adult. Whatever he was supposed to teach his son should have taken place during his childhood. He can't blame somebody else for what he didn't teach. Now his son's decisions and the consequences of those decisions are all his.

Parents have a tendency at any given moment to think and make plans as though whatever stage their child is in will go on forever. They build a play structure in the backyard for their toddler, not realizing that in the blink of an eye she'll have outgrown it and want a batting cage.

Parents have to constantly adjust to their child's progress and needs:

- *No longer need you daily.* For many years your kids need your attention and care every single day. But eventually they will outgrow that. You may still see them every day, but they start to become self-sufficient and no longer ask you about or for something every day. You have to start well in advance to prepare them for that time, and to prepare yourself for that time too.

- *Carving their own identity.* In the latter years of childhood, your kids will feel compelled to create their own identity and distinguish themselves from you. This doesn't mean they are rejecting you as their parent or no longer love you. The pulling away and separating is an important part of the process of preparing to leave the nest.

- *Allow them to fail.* As legendary UCLA basketball coach John Wooden said, "The worst thing you can do for someone is something they can do for themself." As your children pull away you must allow them to do things for themselves on their own. You have to be willing to allow them to fail. You have to learn to resist the impulse to rush in to rescue them.

- *Can't make it up later.* Don't wait until your kids start separating from you to develop close relationships with them. Whatever you did prior to them pulling away is largely what you will take into the future. If you don't have strong bonds with your kids in their youth, don't count on being close during the adult years.

- *Always your child.* Even adults often become kids again when they are with their parents. You sometimes see this at emotional family events such as weddings. Adult sons and daughters will sometimes revert back into their child-adult relationships with their parents. "Mom, you know I don't like my vegetables to touch the other food on my plate!"

At a certain point you have to stop trying to control them and say, "As I see it, here are your options, but it is your choice, and I will respect your decision." There will be swings between your children following your example and doing the opposite to demonstrate their independence.

You "can't stop them". But, then again, why would you want to? For the rest of your life, they'll always be your kids, and you'll always be their parents. And even though they are adults they'll still want your advice on certain decisions. Either consciously or subconsciously, they'll always seek your love and approval.

## Dig Back Out

"You know, you're fucking stupid." Harold shouted at Nick, his old college buddy, as a police officer slowly drove away. Harold had schmoozed the policeman into letting Nick go after Nick had been stopped for speeding before becoming belligerent. "First of all, that cop has twice kept this house from being ripped off. Happens to be a hell of a guy. And you..."

Harold struggled to get the words out. He and Nick were part of a group of old college friends who hadn't seen each other in a long time, as depicted in the movie *The Big Chill*. Their initial friendships were forged 15 years ago when they were all at identical stages in their lives in college. Now they were in different places. Nick was still a free spirit with no wife, kids, or obligations. Harold, on the other hand, owned a business and a magnificent historic mansion and was married with young kids.

"Is jail another experience you want to try? See what that's like?" Harold muttered, trying to keep the top on his anger, "You know, I live here. This place means something to me. I'm dug in. I don't need this shit."

When you got married and first had kids, you dug in deep, like Harold. Now your kids are nearly grown and don't need you all the time. It is time for you to let go and reflect on the child-raising years.

When parents have their first child the instinct to nest is very strong. Friends have to allow new parents to go off with their mate and baby and have the time and privacy they need. Sure, when everyone was together in college, like the classmates from the *Big Chill*, they thought these days of being together all the time would go on forever. But they don't. Everyone went their separate ways and is in a different phase of life now.

- *When you have your first child, it can seem to the outside world that you disappeared for about five years.* And at the other end, when your last kid leaves home, you may go into depression for a year.

- *When you have your first child you fall in love with them.* As your children near adulthood, you need to transfer your love back to your spouse or the marriage may not survive.

- *Your children learn a lot from you, but you also learn a lot from being a parent.* You're now more compassionate with other people. It becomes possible to see each person as someone's son or daughter.

What everyone treasures about being a new parent is all the little moments and firsts. The first diaper, the first feeding, the first steps, the first words. The simplest things are the sweetest.

We've all seen over the years famous Hollywood leading men—like Cary Grant or Warren Beatty or George Clooney—go for decades as proud 'confirmed bachelors with no kids.' Clooney famously said that being an uncle was sufficient for him and he had no reason to need children "of his own loins." Then, like clockwork, in their 50s these stars get married, and you see them on talk shows, educating the world about the joys of burping their kid or how loud she farted. As though they invented parenthood, and nobody else has ever experienced all of that. And that's beautiful. That's wonderful. Because the fulfillment they are embracing could not be more true.

Young kids can be very hard on your work, your marriage, your mission, and your relationships with friends and family due to the time commitment they require. And they're very expensive. But they brought out the best in you. Raising them was an amazingly rewarding project that you accomplished together with them. And now you have to let them go off on their own and start to treat them more like teammates. The adults of a family are a team that helps one another with their projects, missions, legacies, and of course with the next generation.

Go ahead and mourn the end of this era when your last kid leaves home. And gather the strength to keep moving forward.

## Transcending Your Teachings

"My son," D'Artagnan's father said to him as he prepared to leave the family farm on horseback to seek adventures as a musketeer, "You are young. You ought to be brave for two reasons: the first is that you are a Gascon, and the second is that you are my son. Never fear quarrels, but seek adventures. I have taught you how to handle a sword. You have thews of iron, a wrist of steel. Fight on all occasions.... I have nothing to give you, my son, but fifteen crowns, my horse, and the counsel you have just heard."

So begins Alexandre Dumas's classic novel, *The Three Musketeers*. D'Artagnan follows his father's counsel and unfortunately, within just a day of arriving in Paris, he has already insulted and been challenged to a duel by each of France's three greatest swordsmen, the King's elite musketeers Athos, Porthos, and Aramis. His father had done the best he could with limited resources to raise D'Artagnan and teach him to be daring and how to fight with a sword, but his country teachings were inadequate to prepare him for the intrigue of 17$^{th}$ century Paris life.

*The Three Musketeers* essentially chronicles D'Artagnan's adventures under the tutelage of the three mischievous, hard-drinking, gambling, carousing, larger-than-life musketeers, who each mentor him in different areas. They teach D'Artagnan to go beyond what he learned from his parents, how to navigate the politics and dangers of court life, and initiate him into their military order. They mold him into a chivalrous swordsman, fighting for justice rather than for his own personal glory. Eventually, after helping avert a plot to embarrass the queen, D'Artagnan is commissioned a musketeer and is able to join his three friends as a full-fledged member of the King's elite guard.

All children enter adulthood with the shadows of their parents, teachers, and coaches towering unseen and unnoticed behind them. Eventually your kids will come to the realization that, like D'Artagnan's father, you loved them, you had their best interests at heart, and you did the best you could for them. But now they must keep going and transcend your teachings.

Perhaps the greatest example of a wise and caring parent who nonetheless must be transcended is Forrest Gump's mother. Throughout his childhood, Forrest had been able to go to Mama Gump whenever he was confused or didn't know what to do next. And for the first two hours of *Forrest Gump*, his mother filled him up with amazing nuggets of wisdom. Everything from "life is like a box of chocolates" to "you are the same as everyone else" to "stupid is as stupid does."

But now, as an adult, he asked, "Mama, what's my destiny?" And for the first time, she didn't offer her son an answer. Mama Gump told Forrest, with dewy eyes and a kind smile, "You're going to have to figure that out for yourself." Forrest was no longer a boy. He was a man now. An All-American football player. A war hero. An Olympic ping pong champion. And even a Fortune 500 company owner. Forrest was grown and had surpassed Mama and her teachings. It was time for him to figure out a few things for himself.

When D'Artagnan and Forrest and all other kids were growing up, they thought adults knew everything. At a certain time in life, parents, coaches, teachers, and bosses really can help kids out with pretty much any challenge that comes along. But every kid finally has to go beyond. They will hang onto many truths you taught them. But they will discard some too in favor of new truths they will discover for themselves. At times they will think back kindly on the sacrifices you made in raising them and regret some of the aggravations they caused you. And at other times they will shake their heads as they think how outdated or wrongheaded some of your ideas were.

We all see our parents as monolithic. We believe subconsciously that they'll always be around, and always with us. And then, finally, they are no longer there.

## No Questions Asked

"I don't know who you are. I don't know what you want," said Bryan Mills calmly to the Albanian kidnapper on the phone, "I don't have money. But what I do have are a very particular set of skills." You almost have to feel sorry for criminals foolish enough to kidnap the daughter of Bryan Mills, a former CIA operative played by Liam Neeson in *Taken*, and its sequels. Because he will always come running to the rescue, no questions asked—and destroy you and your gang of thugs singlehandedly!

And that is your role too, now that your kids are grown. They will rely on you, your skills, and your resources in times of urgent need. You are the only people your children can really depend on to come running, no questions asked, when it really counts.

You have to maintain your relationships with your children and continue to keep an eye on them and their families even after they are grown:

- *What do they need?* Instead of asking your grown kids, "Do you want my help?" be perceptive and do a little detective work. Figure out what they need, and offer it. Let them choose whether to accept your offer. It can be embarrassing for your adult kids to ask for help.

- *Assistance or criticism?* Don't offer to help if your offer is the sugar coating around a criticism. What is your real objective when you ask one of your grown kids if they'd like to borrow some money to paint the house? To finance the project or to tell your daughter the front of her house looks terrible? Offer to help *only* to help.

- *Be the peacekeeper.* When your kids were living under your roof and there were squabbles, it was difficult sometimes to not get carried away with the emotion of the moment. Now it is your job to help steer the various members of the family away from arguments and conflicts and help defuse them when they arise.

- *The "family diamond mine."* If you can, try to set up a trust with some money in it, or a family business or an investment property, that can assist the generations of your family financially a little bit and provide a mechanism for staying connected. Ensure the governance documents are clear and fair and allow for exits.

The proof that any of us at any age would love to have a Mama Bear or a Papa Bear—a totally devoted parent with specialized skills who can help us in a crisis—is demonstrated by the impressive run Liam Neeson has had essentially playing that same capable father character in half a dozen films since starring in *Taken* in 2008. As *Esquire* magazine says, "Neeson has largely taken over from Harrison Ford the "family in jeopardy" genre on the strength of that single scene [with the warning to the kidnapper about his formidable skills]." His *Taken* films have grossed nearly a billion dollars.

Beyond helping our children in an emergency, recognize also that nobody knows how to tackle the big firsts in life like buying a house, negotiating with a boss for a raise, or planning a wedding until they've done it. And this is where they may need deeply personal advice from someone they can really trust. We must keep in mind that our adult children are still maturing mentally until the age of 25 or so, which is well into the adventure stage of life. During these years when they are part child and part adult, the likelihood is high that they will inadvertently bring some kind of significant problem or true crisis upon themselves. And they may need our assistance to resolve it.

"You don't remember me," Bryan Mills told the gang of Albanian thugs whose safe house he had infiltrated by the end of *Taken*. "We spoke on the phone ten days ago. I told you I would find you." Bryan Mills looks after his daughter even though she's an adult. We all should too.

## Gratitude Across Generations

"Mom and Dad, I've decided to become a motorcycle daredevil. I think a lot of Evel Knievel's records are ripe for being broken. I'm going to start by jumping over a hundred school buses lit on fire. And don't try to talk me out of it. It's *my* life. I can do whatever I want." As your own children enter the adventure stage of life, imagine if one of them came to you to announce a high risk and possibly ill-conceived plan for the future.

What would you think? What would you say? Probably something like, "Yes, it is your life. Yes, you have to make your own choices. But I want to remind you that your father and I, your siblings, and your grandparents love you. And because of that, we have all made a significant investment of energy and time in you. We don't want to see any harm come to you that can be avoided. Please don't live recklessly and treat the sacrifices we've made for you carelessly."

Now that your kids are grown, that means you've taken your family through a full generation. If you haven't already, it is time to thank earlier generations of family for the sacrifices they made for you. You aren't obligated to thank them. They aren't expecting you to thank them. But you should still thank them anyway. Today!

- *Thank your parents.* Every little effort your parents made for you left a small blemish or dent on them. Recognize that the age you see on them now is in part due to the impact of their sacrifice. "Mom and Dad, I won the lottery by having you as my parents. I'm grateful for who you helped me become and for everything I've been able to accomplish thanks to your support. I love you."
- *Thank your siblings.* "We did it! There's no way I could have made

it without your support, my brothers and sisters. You helped me with my homework, you taught me how to doorbell ditch our neighbors, you gave me rides, and you stuck up for me when I teased those big kids. Mom and Dad made us, but we helped make a great family together. Thank you for the love you gave me."

- *Thank aunts, uncles, and grandparents.* The best way to show gratitude and love to your other elder relatives is simply to check in on them. Call them or visit them. Ask them how they are doing. Let them tell you about their aches and pains. Allow them to share stories about the way things used to be. Listen attentively to any wisdom they have for you, and enjoy it.

Your family is everything. Let love continue to circulate through the generations of your family rather than letting it be unreciprocated and dissipate. You received so much from your family when you were young. Now it is time for you to give thanks for all you received and to witness your kids produce the next generation.

By embracing and experiencing each of the five life stages we can live a continuously fulfilling life. The family stage of life overlaps with the mission stage, as does the tribe stage, as shown on the diagram below. The relationships we develop within our families and tribes as we execute our missions give life much of its richness.

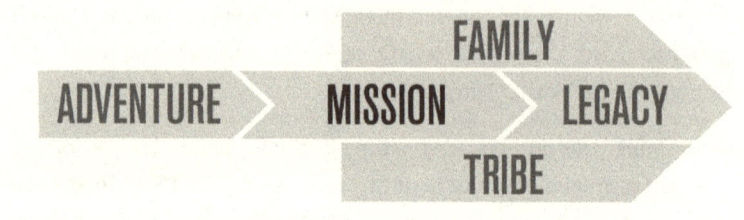

ADVENTURE > MISSION / FAMILY / TRIBE > LEGACY

# 4. LEAD TRIBE

### Tribes in Ancient Times

The islanders lashed ropes made from braided strips of palm fronds around the thick neck and torso of the 30-foot-tall statue, which was laying on its back. They were high up on the side of the volcano, in the quarry. The tribe's five best stoneworkers had been coming here every day for almost two years, carving the enormous statue with handheld rock chisels. But now it was going to take all 80 members of the tribe to release the volcanic tuff statue from the hillside quarry and prop it upright so it could be moved. They had palm-tree rollers and wooden levers ready. It was the most elaborate mission this generation of the tribe had ever undertaken. The new chieftain had a solemn duty to honor their beloved fallen chieftain by overseeing the carving of this massive 50-ton statue in his likeness, and then transport it almost a mile down to the coast. There it would take its place alongside the other *moai* on a raised platform that had been there for centuries, and would watch over the tribe for eternity. And here these magnificent statues, known only to the inhabits of this Polynesian island of *Rapa Nui,* would stand, until it was discovered on Easter, 1722, by European explorers. Thereafter, it became known to the world as Easter Island.

Loosely speaking, a "tribe" is a group of between 30 and 100 people united by a common mission that is overseen by their chieftain. A tribe is large enough that members can each specialize and become adept at a specific task: fishing, building huts, farming, carving statues, etc. But the tribe is also small enough that all the members are able to know and hold one another accountable for their actions. Groups smaller than 30 tend to function more like families, with less specialization and everyone needing to be able to do a bit of everything. And with groups larger than 100 people, it becomes difficult for everyone to know one another. Factions tend to form, causing the group to become unstable and split apart.

In prehistoric times necessity required everyone to live in tribes:

- Tribes were successful families that grew into larger groups but remained connected by kinship and intermarriage.
- A person had to be a member of a tribe in order to survive famine, disasters, predators, disease, and war.
- Tribe members spent most of their time securing food, fighting with competing tribes, and worshipping their ancestors.
- Boys went with the tribesmen to learn to hunt and fight. Girls went with the tribeswomen to learn how to gather and prepare food.
- Self-worth was defined by helping to make the tribe powerful rather than by pursuing success as an individual.
- The tribe distinguished itself by fighting with other tribes, taking their resources, and destroying their idols or temples.
- Shamans or medicine men could use trances or special substances to see the future, answer the chieftain's questions, or heal injuries.
- The chieftain was responsible for reinforcing the legends of the tribe's victories, and for leading the tribe in executing its mission.
- The tribe gave offerings to make their ancestors comfortable in the spirit world. In return, the dead provided fertility and good fortune.
- There was no "heaven." Immortality could only be found by ensuring the tribe survived and remaining connected to it.

In our modern world, people work in tribes *by choice* to earn income, rather than live in tribes *by necessity* in order to survive. Now that you've spent the time necessary to conceptualize and establish your mission, it is time to move on to the next stage. You must construct a tribe around your mission and take on the duties that go with serving as its chieftain.

## The Tribal Chieftain

Buntek "Ted" Ngoy fled the genocide of the brutal Khmer Rouge in Cambodia and emigrated to California in 1975. While working at a gas station he noticed a thriving donut shop across the street and asked how he could get involved in the business. He was directed to Winchell's training program. Winchell's was the largest donut chain in California at that time. As a trainee he learned all aspects of shop operations and how to make every kind of donut on the menu before being given a store to manage. He proved to be a quick study and a capable manager and began his mission of building a donut empire, as detailed in his book *The Donut King*.

Within a year Ngoy had learned the ropes and saved enough money to buy a poorly performing donut shop with a loan from the seller. Under the name Christy's Donuts and with his attention to cleanliness and by baking fresh donuts throughout the day rather than just once in the morning, he made it successful. Soon he began recruiting nieces, nephews, and other Cambodian immigrants to help him run dozens of additional shops he purchased. Ngoy next continued his expansion by recruiting other political refugees from Cambodia and helped them establish residency in the United States. He leased donut shops to them so they could support their families. He achieved his mission and became both the self-proclaimed Donut King of California and a prominent leader with the Cambodian-American community.

A chieftain is the leader of a tribe. In modern times a "chieftain," as the term is used in these pages, forms a tribe in order to obtain assistance from people they trust in executing their mission on a larger scale than they could on their own. Their personal mission becomes the tribe's mission. They are responsible for directing and overseeing the activities of their tribe's members. Additionally, they become responsible for inspiring their tribe and providing members an opportunity to earn income, learn skills, and have more autonomy than they otherwise would if they worked for an institution.

A person's mission is highly unique and individualized, as is the tribe's mission. And with tribal missions taking many different forms, it also follows that there are many types of chieftains. Some want to maximize an existing product, like Ngoy did. Some are more artistic. Some are born glad-handers. And some are charismatic wheeler-dealers. But they all tend to have certain things in common:

- *Chieftains are hard workers* and are willing to perform any tribal task, even if it isn't glamorous. They'll bake donuts all day if needed.

- *Chieftains have a deep desire for their tribe to be self-sufficient.* They are experts at finding ways to maximize their resources so that their customers, allies, vendors, etc., aren't able to tell them what to do.

- *Chieftains are perceptive and good at anticipating.* Rather than reacting to situations after they become a problem like their tribe members might, they excel at staying a step ahead of problems.

- *Chieftains may be reserved or they may be outgoing*, but they genuinely care about their people, and they telegraph this care through their actions. This makes them magnetic to tribal members.

- *Chieftains have a deep desire to accomplish the tribal mission*, and are incredibly persistent and resilient in executing it. Over time they become masters of learning to turn setbacks into triumphs.

The most successful chieftains win over tribespeople by showing them that through helping achieve the chieftain's tribal mission, they will obtain what they want too—namely, a piece of something they believe in. They may also receive income to support their families and skills and knowledge they can ultimately take with them to pursue their own missions, build their own tribe, and eventually become a chieftain themselves.

## Leadership vs. Management

"Chanel insisted upon using a massive quantity of jasmine for one simple reason...jasmine petals were impossibly expensive," wrote Rhonda Garelick in her book, *Mademoiselle*. Coco Chanel wanted to create "the most expensive perfume in the world."

By 1920, when she set her mind on creating a signature perfume, Coco Chanel was already a successful 37-year-old fashion designer and entrepreneur in France. She was a natural commander and assembled a tribe of designers, seamstresses, and salespeople around her, indoctrinating them to her incredibly high standards of product quality and customer service.

For years she had raided her boyfriends' closets for their polo, tennis, and hunting togs, adapting them into minimalistic, comfortable clothing for women, including the first commercially available women's pants and bathing suits. Her casual designs caused a sensation in an era in which women wore dresses and corsets for all occasions. Chanel created an athletic and youthful aesthetic that has endured for over a century.

She recruited Ernest Beaux, who had been the perfumer for Russian tsars, to join her tribe as her chief perfumer. Together, working tirelessly in the laboratory, they created something unique and iconic. It was the first perfume made from all jasmine (rather than blending flowers to reduce costs). It was the first perfume named after a person (Chanel herself) rather than given a poetic name. It was the first perfume to be numbered—Chanel No. 5. And it was the first perfume to be bottled in an angular, minimalistic, geometric bottle (modeled after her boyfriend's vodka flask) rather than in a decorative flacon.

Chanel No. 5 has been the world's top selling perfume for over a century. And it made Coco Chanel a billionaire. With all the resources Chanel controlled, she could have chosen to outsource and *manage* its design and production. But she instead chose to *lead* every aspect of the creation and marketing of her namesake perfume.

In our modern world, discussions about leadership often focus on describing the tasks a leader must perform and the techniques and strategies for accomplishing those tasks, rather than on the larger *purpose* of leadership. This is a result of confusing *leaders* and *managers*. Leadership is a mindset and is distinct from management, which is a set of skills. Managers are responsible for overseeing tasks. Leaders are responsible for developing, overseeing, and providing for people.

Managers use the resources and the subordinates assigned to them to complete projects and meet goals they have been ordered to carry out by their superiors. Leaders of tribes, a.k.a. chieftains, determine the mission, then execute the mission by working together with the tribal members they have assembled. People instinctively dislike feeling as though they are being *managed*, because it makes them feel like cogs in a machine rather than human beings. They want to be *led* toward the accomplishment of a mission they feel is important and in which they have a stake.

Managers in committees agree on safe ideas for products with low-risk names. It takes a leader like Chanel to come up with an original and unique idea that remains on top for a century. Missions are human endeavors. We all want to work with an aggressive, nimble, creative, and caring leader with a mission that speaks to us, such as "creating the world's finest perfume." Few of us care to work under a passive, careful manager.

While you are a chieftain, be a leader. And if you should be fortunate enough to ultimately grow your tribe into an institution, remain a leader, and ensure the people working with you act as leaders. Organizations that become filled with managers who view themselves as responsible for tasks, projects, and goals, but not for developing people or moving a mission forward, will frequently end up having no lasting internal strength or cohesion.

## Under Your Protection

Much the Miller's Son ran over to the deer he had just felled with his bow. As he crouched to begin cleaning it, knife in hand, he heard the sound of horses. In an instant he was surrounded by the royal gamekeeper and two of his men. "You know the penalty for killing a royal deer!" the gamekeeper shouted at Much and raised a wooden club over his head to strike him. Much had thought that he would have been safe this deep in Sherwood Forest, but now he knew he was about to pay for his mistake with his life. Then the air crackled with a whizzing sound and the club flew out of the gamekeeper's hand. An arrow had sent the club flying, and a wave of sweet relief swept over Much. Sure enough, Robin Hood and Will Scarlet galloped in on horseback. The gamekeeper pulled Much to his feet to arrest him.

"Let him go," said Robin. "He is with me. I had him kill that deer."

"The penalty for killing a royal deer is death," he bellowed.

"Really?" Robin smiled, a twinkle in his eye as he pulled an arrow from its quiver, drew it in his bow, and leaned forward in his saddle, pointing it at the gamekeeper's chest all in one smooth motion. "Are there no exceptions?"

The gamekeeper and his men rode off. Robin, Will, and Much laughed and laughed. "Thank god you came along when you did, Robin!"

Robin Hood, with his band of Merry Men, is one of the most legendary examples of a tribe with specialized skills devoted to their cunning, charismatic chieftain and committed to their mission of overthrowing a tyrant who is stealing from their countrymen. Robin understood and lived by an implicit bond with his people. Those who serve the tribe are under the chieftain's protection.

- *One of the people.* No chieftain can be successful by behaving as though they are above or better than the other tribal members. The chieftain's demeanor shows they view themself as part of the tribe, and able to understand the needs and thoughts of the tribespeople.

- *Feed your people first.* The tribal mission comes first, followed by taking care of your people, and then yourself. Tribal members love and reward with loyalty a chieftain who takes care of them and "feeds them first."

- *The virtue of largesse.* In ancient times, one of the chieftain's most important duties was to distribute the fruits of the hunt and the spoils of war fairly among his people. This included giving an extra share to those who had grown old or were injured serving the tribe.

- *Give them the credit.* When the tribe achieves victories, the chieftain is quick to give credit to all the members of the tribe. When there is a setback or a mistake, the chieftain assumes responsibility. A chieftain has no other person to blame.

- *Strength, not perfection.* The tribe wants leadership and strength from the chieftain, not perfection. With a big and important tribal mission will come challenges and miscalculations that everyone has to pitch in and fix. When these occur, the chieftain takes the lead.

There has to be a good balance between carrying out the tribal mission and caring for one's people. With the role of the chieftain will come times of loneliness, confusion, and despair. Chieftains must summon the strength and courage to move the tribe forward with confidence, and with the tribespeople feeling the chieftain's aura of protection around them. The chieftain must perform at his or her best when everything is going to plan or when conditions look bleak.

## The Allure of the Tribe

"Once you got in at Gucci you knew you were set for life," said a young apprentice bag-maker in 1960. Back in those days, Gucci had grown beyond operating as a family enterprise and had been transformed into a tribe. "Each workman was responsible for what he did, and his number went into each bag…. It wasn't like an assembly line where someone did the pockets and someone else did the sleeves." Roberto Gucci said of his tribal members, "We knew each worker by name, and we knew about their children, their problems, their joys. If they needed help to buy a car or put a down payment on a house—they came to us."

While the Gucci brothers formed a leather goods tribe in Italy, two former fraternity brothers, Steve Rubell and Ian Schrager, formed the Studio 54 tribe in New York. After gaining entrepreneurial experience with restaurants and a disco, they vowed to change the world by creating the greatest nightclub of all time. They assembled a tribe of bartenders, waiters, hostesses, bouncers, dancers, and other performers.

On a limited budget and with limited time they put all their energy into converting the former Gallo Opera House into a nightclub where they could host highly theatrical one-of-a-kind events each evening. "It was the greatest mixture of celebrities, weird characters in costume, transvestites and dancers the world has ever seen." The line to get into the club stretched around the block, and the duo "made more money than the Mafia."

The Studio 54 employees had as much fun as the patrons, and in some cases had more clout in society than the celebrity guests, because entrance into the club was so closely guarded by Rubell and his bouncers.

Gucci, in the early days, and Studio 54 (right up to the time it was raided by the FBI for skimming millions of dollars in cash), were both tribes. On the other hand, when Ted Ngoy went to Winchell's to obtain his initial donut training, it wasn't a tribe. Winchell's was an "institution." It was a subsidiary of the Denny's restaurant chain with over 200 stores.

The workers in each Winchell's donut shop mostly only knew each other and not the employees in the other shops. There were corporate-level managers who monitored revenue and came up with companywide promotional ideas, but there was no need for them to meet the shop employees or even all the shop managers.

When the Guccis, Rubell and Schrager, and Ngoy decided to expand their missions and create larger teams around themselves, their friends and families eagerly joined in the tribes—because tribes are alluring:

- *The tribe has a mission that is set internally* by a dynamic and talented chieftain, rather than by receiving orders from afar.

- *Each person in the tribe is expected to be a producer* rather than an intermediary, which gives each member ownership of their work.

- Through working and socializing together, *tribes naturally create situations resulting in members knowing and liking each other.*

- *Tribes cherish their individual members* and bring in people they like and trust, whereas institutions see employees as interchangeable.

Institutions are a great place for a young person like Ngoy to obtain training, experience, relationships, and income they can use later in forming a tribe. But an institution's complexity creates the need for layers of supervisors and elaborate written procedures which may lead to employee frustration. Institutions tend to be slow and deliberate. Tribes are nimble, fast, and opportunistic. They are good vehicles for chieftains who wish to pursue a significant outward expansion of their mission, as Ngoy did with his donut tribe.

## Distilling the Tribal Mission

Phil Knight's athletic-shoe company, Blue Ribbon, had lost its public face, 1970s running sensation Steve Prefontaine, in a tragic car accident that took his life. And the company had narrowly averted bankruptcy after being cleared of suspected fraud by the FBI as a result of inadvertently bouncing some large checks. These two existential threats to Blue Ribbon provoked a lot of soul searching, which Knight wrote about in his book *Shoe Dog*:

"What are we trying to build here? What kind of company do we want to be? Several times in those first months of 1976, I huddled with Hayes and Woodell and Strasser, and over sandwiches and sodas we'd kick around this question of ultimate goals. Money wasn't our aim, we agreed. Money wasn't our end game."

And then, at last, Blue Ribbon's mission came into focus. The new athletic training shoe they had developed, with its patented waffle sole, was a hit with athletes due to its comfort and its unique, colorful swoosh stripes on its sides. Knight had a sudden thought, "People might start wearing this thing to class. And the office. And the grocery store. And throughout their everyday lives."

*That* was the mission. Not creating the ultimate running shoe. Not making money. But turning this new kind of shoe they had poured their lives into developing into something everybody—not just elite athletes training for competitions—could wear every day. And then, a final stroke of inspiration: Knight had the factories start making the shoes in blue so they would match with jeans. Sales took off immediately. "Blue Ribbon, we decided, had run its course. We would have to incorporate as Nike, Inc."

If Phil Knight had been a brand manager at Adidas or Tiger or another athletic shoe company in the 1970s that was of institutional size, some core group of senior leaders in a skyscraper somewhere would have told him what shoe he could or couldn't bring to market. But tribes, like Blue Ribbon, are different. Tribes have missions that are internally generated by a chieftain, like Knight, and are kicked around, modified, and improved through the consensus of the group. A tribe does not wait for orders or approval from some outside committee to formulate and execute its mission. The tribe has the leeway to have its chieftain act on a hunch and tell the factory to make blue shoes.

The tribe's process of distilling its mission and acting upon it is both informal and collegial:

- *The chieftain's initiative.* The chieftain put the tribe together around his or her personal mission. So the chieftain must take the initiative in evolving the tribe's mission. Nothing happens until they gather their people to brainstorm.

- *One mission.* A tribe that has more than one mission doesn't have a mission. The tribe must adapt the chieftain's personal mission into a singular mission that galvanizes and motivates the tribe. This begins by defining it in a single sentence understood by all.

- *Analyze the obstacles.* Once the tribal mission has been distilled, the next step is identifying any impediments to its execution followed by formulating a plan for eliminating or neutralizing these obstacles. The next step is executing the mission, refining it as needed.

As soon as Knight and his tribe had improved and distilled their mission, Blue Ribbon went from many years of slow, steady growth to becoming the true business juggernaut we know today as Nike. Their comfortable and attractive shoes upended the custom of that era of wearing athletic shoes only for sports. When the members of a tribe clearly know its mission, the world provides opportunities for the mission to be achieved.

## Teach and Train Your People

"I don't clean toilets," said Rod, the new busboy, taking a step back and shaking his head. Lyndall, holding a bottle of Lysol and long rubber gloves, moved toward him. "You don't clean toilets?" she asked with her Australian lilt and a gleam in her eye. "Well, *I* do." She went right past him into the bathroom, bent down, and started scrubbing. Rod stood in the doorway watching with wide eyes, not knowing what to do next.

Throughout the 1980s, Lyndall Radeczki and her husband, Michael, an Austrian pastry chef, owned and operated the Vienna Café together in La Jolla, California. They were bosses that did things that weren't always familiar to their American employees. "Okay, Lyndall, I'll do the rest," Rod said with a croak in his voice. "No, Rod, just watch. I'm never going to ask you to do something I haven't done a thousand times myself." Michael and the rest of the team muffled their laughter a bit, knowing it was just part of the training and initiation process. They knew Lyndall was probably chuckling inside too.

Lyndall finished cleaning, restocking, and mopping the bathroom before telling Rod to go back to clearing tables, refilling water glasses, and cleaning dishes. When the lunch rush ended Michael called out to Rod in his thick accent, "So, what are you eating for your lunch today, Rod?" After a pause Rod said, "I'm not really too hungry right now, Mike." Michael's eyes opened wide. "Rod, my name is Michael. And when a person is working for me, I am not only paying them, I am cooking for them. You are never telling a chef you are not hungry." Now Lyndall chimed in, "Rod, pick something off our menu. You're a hard worker, and I need you to keep up your energy. And you'll have to know the whole menu by the time I promote you to waiter so you can tell our customers when they ask you what's good to eat here."

A gourmet restaurant like the Vienna Café, with waiters, busboys, hostesses, cooks, bakers, and cashiers, is another type of enterprise that runs like a tribe. Big chain restaurants have elaborate procedure manuals. Independent restaurants, on the other hand, typically have a strong-willed chieftain, like Lyndall. A chieftain with a clear vision for how every aspect of the restaurant must run and who trains everyone to her level of detail.

- *Show what is expected.* Recruiting good people with the right skills is just a start. Tribes don't have operations manuals, so the chieftain must continuously demonstrate their expectations. Lyndall showed her people the techniques for moving as many patrons as possible through the café with everyone feeling cared for and not rushed.

- *Distinguish between abilities.* Lyndall taught the busboys to wash dishes fast without breaking glasses. She taught the cashiers to keep the bills facing the same way to avoid mistakes. She taught the waiters to make the meal a pleasant experience for the guests. She required excellence from each according to age, ability, and role.

- *Patiently layering lessons.* She required everyone to work at full speed when the café was busy, and to deep clean everything when it was slow. This continuous hard work mentality took time to internalize. Lyndall was patient in finding little ways to prod and motivate the team to always be working to keep the café humming.

- *Model the tribe's attitude.* Lyndall was proud of the food and service at the Vienna Café, and she loved a good laugh. This showed in her posture and the musical tone of her voice. It was fun to be there, and nobody wanted to miss a day of work. Everyone she hired eventually adopted her confident and boisterous demeanor.

Teaching your tribe never ends. Some people are self-motivated. Some people need a pat on the back. Some people need a poke in the ribs. There's always a rookie to train, or a veteran being promoted. Let even cleaning a toilet be an opportunity to teach.

## Playing Without Restrictions

"Now, if you'll excuse me, I'm going to go on an overnight drunk, and in ten days I'm going to set out to find the shark that ate my friend and destroy it," said Steve Zissou to the crew of his oceanographic research vessel, the *Belafonte*. "Anyone who wants to tag along is more than welcome."

Steve Zissou doesn't issue orders to the tribe of talented eccentrics that has coalesced around him. Rather, he has put an irresistible mission in front of them and the opportunity to participate in it. In *The Life Aquatic With Steve Zissou*, a loving cinematic homage to Jacques Cousteau, we see the ultimate tribe of brilliant specialists who are free to be themselves: Eleanor Zissou (Steve's wealthy wife and the real brains of the operation), Klaus Daimler (German first mate), Pele Dos Santos (Brazilian demolition expert), Vikram Ray (Indian cameraman), Bobby Ogata (Japanese frogman), Vladimir Wolodarsky (Russian soundtrack composer), a cadre of unpaid interns from the University of North Alaska, and many others. Each has their own area of expertise plus other areas they choose to dabble in. And each wears a slightly different variation of Zissou's red beanie and powder-blue nautical uniform.

Some chieftains, especially new ones, think it is their job to give orders and do most of the thinking for the tribe. But it takes a lot of effort to constantly tell everyone exactly what they need to do. As a chieftain becomes more seasoned, they realize that giving their people as much freedom as possible to think for themselves is better for all.

- Rather than turning your tribespeople into copies of you, *let them be themselves*. The tribe needs genuine, unique people.

- Give tribal members *latitude to create or expand their role* within the tribe. Then they'll buy into the responsibilities that go with it.

- Try to help your people *figure out for themselves* what they should do. That makes them better decision-makers when it really matters.

- When you limit your people, they put a lot of energy into bending your rules. *Harness that energy* instead by giving them freedom.

- Only put *hard limits* on what your tribal members can do when you feel they are *moving in opposition to the mission*.

Remember, your people aren't perfect. Most of them are with you because of certain talents, skills, and attributes they have for doing specific things that benefit the tribe. You can't get upset if they can't perform a task that isn't in their wheelhouse. A tyrannical boss, like a Silicon Valley tech tycoon, expects everyone to be able to do everything at his one-in-a-million-genius level. But that's the opposite of how tribes work. Tribe members specialize for the tribe's benefit. Don't expect your accountant to also be your salesperson, or your best pitcher to also be your best hitter.

"I believe in freedom. I don't believe in overmanaging. I believe in players being themselves, playing without restrictions. The more you restrict freedom, the more you restrict creativity," said Joe Maddon after winning the World Series as the manager of the Chicago Cubs. "The value of connecting with people exceeded whatever could be gained from ordering them around."

For you as the chieftain to accomplish an extraordinary mission, you have to surround yourself with tribespeople who are each extraordinary in different ways. That is how they are able to help you and help each other, so all of you together are able to execute the mission.

If you fill the tribe with people who can only take orders, the tribe's mission will never evolve beyond you, and the tribe will never thrive. Attract smart, original people with good, creative ideas. Then give them the freedom needed to help grow the tribe and expand the tribal mission.

## Absorb Uncertainty

"It was crazy," said Francis Ford Coppola of filming *Apocalypse Now*. "We were in the jungle. There were too many of us. We had access to too much money. Too much equipment. And little by little we went insane." Coppola's mission was to make the first film to win the Nobel Prize. But the film nearly bankrupted him and almost destroyed his career.

Coppola had gone to the Philippines in 1976 with his production team to shoot *Apocalypse Now*, which was loosely based on the novel *Heart of Darkness* by Joseph Conrad. Although set in the Vietnam War, the film wasn't about the war. It was about a journey up a river, searching for the elusive Colonel Kurtz, who has "gone native" and become insane.

From the beginning the film and its production were plagued by setbacks, uncertainties, and weather delays. The film quickly ran over budget due to elaborate helicopter sequences and the construction of a lost city built out of 300-pound blocks. Marlon Brando, charging $1 million per week, argued endlessly about the script and had become so overweight that only his face is shown in the film. And lead actor Martin Sheen suffered a heart attack during filming, halting production for weeks.

The size of the production continued to expand, and Coppola bravely absorbed the conflict and challenges that went with it, keeping his production tribespeople on task. Like his crew, most people's greatest fears are of being put in situations they can't control, being exposed to risks they can't quantify, or being placed in circumstances that appear to be worsening.

One of a chieftain's primary roles is to absorb this uncertainty to create insulation and stability for the tribe. Chieftains, too, are anxious in a crisis situation, but they don't show their fears. They focus their energy on resolving the crisis rather than worrying or complaining.

- *Don't blame bad luck.* A chieftain can't blame unknowns or bad luck for leading the tribe into an uncomfortable or dangerous situation. Excuses will ring hollow to the members of the tribe. A chieftain has to anticipate unfavorable breaks and find ways to overcome them.

- *Explain the sacrifices.* The chieftain must not misrepresent the severity of the situation. Instead, they explain clearly and confidently that eventually the emergency will be resolved and prosperity restored. Tribe members will accept months or years of toil and sacrifices if they have confidence in the chieftain's plan.

- *Unrest vs. mutiny.* Unrest is inevitable and can be managed or even turned into an advantage. Mutiny must be dealt with immediately and severely. Unrest can grow into mutiny if the chieftain does not keep the tribe busy taking necessary action to overcome the crisis.

Coppola's wife, Eleanor Coppola used footage she had taken for marketing purposes to later create *Hearts of Darkness: A Filmmaker's Apocalypse* about the making of *Apocalypse Now*. She said, "It's scary to see someone you love go into the center of himself and confront his fears. Fear of failure. Fear of death. Fear of going insane." But ultimately, she said, all he could do was go through all that uncertainty and come out on the other side. Which Coppola did, with his film winning the Palm d'Or at Cannes in 1979.

There will always be a crisis to solve; and almost always, a solution appears just in time. Members of the tribe will never really understand—until they become chieftains themselves—just how much effort it requires to absorb uncertainty and provide a secure envelope in which the entire tribe can operate and make continued progress as it travels forward through time.

## Tell Beautiful Stories

Walt Disney won an Academy Award in 1933 for producing the *Three Little Pigs*, an animated short. "Of all the things I've ever done," Disney said, "I'd like to be remembered as a storyteller." His Disney Brothers Studios began the production of the world's first feature-length animated movie in full color and sound, *Snow White and the Seven Dwarfs*. The project was known around Hollywood as "Disney's Folly" during its production, and he had to mortgage his house to complete it. Disney focused on the relationship between the queen and Snow White and made it as realistic and dramatic as possible. The movie was a critical hit and the most financially successful movie of 1938 and ushered in the golden age of animated storytelling.

Storytelling is essential to leading the tribe, because logic, reason, and numbers are not enough to persuade a person to commit themself to a tribe and its mission. Facts, intellect, and analysis each has its place, but we prefer stories about people who take big risks to pursue a deeply personal objective. Chieftains inspire their people via an emotional connection.

Who would you be more inclined to support if you had a hundred dollars to invest? A 26-year-old female entrepreneur offering you a 10-percent annual return opportunity to invest in her commodity household products business? Or, a sick and lonely kid who was an ugly duckling with no friends and was frequently hospitalized due to her allergies but grew up to become one of the world's most beautiful and talented actresses and launched a company providing safe, affordable, organic household products to help parents?

In either case you'd be investing in Jessica Alba and The Honest Company, which she launched and is now valued at over a billion dollars.

Persuading one's people with well-crafted stories is a key skill that chieftains must develop:

- *A pattern-seeking animal.* Man is a pattern-seeking, storytelling animal. Parents teach their young children by telling them stories. It is a pervasive human drive to want to impose meaning on the mysteries of life by creating interesting narratives that can provide explanation. Mythology predates factual human history.

- *Emulate the master storytellers.* Make your stories "crackle with energy," like writer Charles Bukowski. Pick words that sound smooth and interesting in the listener's ear like Jerry Seinfeld does in his stand-up routines. And use Hemingway's "iceberg approach" of lacing a story with a few evocative details on a subject you're an expert in and let the listener subconsciously feel the weight of the rest of your knowledge lying below the surface.

- *Desire and passion blocked by obstacles.* All good stories need conflict. Tell your people an epic story about the tribe. Describe with foreboding all the obstacles that are preventing the tribe from accomplishing its mission. Describe everyone's talents and flaws. Describe all the grueling work you will all have to do to get to a final victory. Everyone loves to sacrifice in exchange for shared success.

These techniques make a story persuasive at a gut level, whereas logical arguments and facts first have to be analyzed by the listener.

People think they want facts, logic, and truth. But in reality, we all want to hear beautiful and well-told stories even if at some level we know that minor details have been streamlined, combined, or embellished. You can shoehorn a story into a few minutes, but everyone prefers a campfire storyteller who takes the time to put a lot of plotlines and characters in motion then somehow pulls them all back in for a satisfying conclusion.

When telling a story, it's okay to take a few liberties with the sequence of events and the outlandishness of the characters. You're not writing a history book. If someone challenges you, simply say, "It's a *story*."

## Collect Good People

"You don't want a ballplayer, you want a stable pony!" shouted Crash Davis, the lovable catcher in the movie *Bull Durham*. After 12 years as a minor leaguer, his contract had been purchased by the Durham Bulls. On this day, he was meeting the manager and staff. Little did he know he had only been procured for one reason: to use his veteran knowledge of the game to help the team groom their young, undisciplined pitching prospect, Nuke Laloosh, into a professional. "I quit!" said Crash. He walked out of the manager's office and slammed the door. He waited a minute outside. Then another minute. Nobody came out to try to stop him from leaving. He went back in and smiled, "When's the first game?"

Professional baseball and football teams are perhaps the ultimate example of tribes that have very specific personnel needs. People enter and leave the tribe all the time. Here are some suggestions for evaluating and recruiting the people your tribe needs:

- *Gather information.* When recruiting new members to the tribe, yes, you want to be relaxed and sociable. But your goal is to gather useful information, not shoot the breeze or brag about your tribe. Is this recruit likeable and someone you can trust? What matters to them? What are their insecurities? What are their goals?

- *Collect good people.* The tribe is like a life raft at sea or a foxhole in a war. It is too small to share with anyone who isn't motivated, smart, hardworking, and a person of good character. Rather than hiring someone with the skills you need and tolerating their lapses, instead disqualify from consideration anyone without integrity.

- *Hire experience and knowledge.* Sure, you can recruit family members and friends because you trust them and hope they can develop skills quickly. But generally speaking, you can better serve the interests of the tribe and its mission by bringing in people who already have the experience and skills the tribe needs. The Bulls hired Crash Davis not just to catch for Nuke, but also to room with him on road games so Nuke was fully immersed in Davis's knowledge.

- *A wide range of personalities.* There are a lot of different roles and personalities within a tribe. Catchers see the world differently than pitchers do. That's no problem as long as everyone understands their own role and has an appreciation of how it works with the roles of the other tribe members to accomplish the tribal mission.

- *Look for dedication.* Be like the manager who left Crash Davis cooling off by himself outside his office. Don't bring someone into the tribe if they need coaxing. Don't bring someone into the tribe who just wants to collect a paycheck. Don't bring someone into the tribe who will jump ship as soon as something better comes along. Instead, bring someone in who finds compelling the tribe's mission and their role in accomplishing that mission.

You want people in the tribe like Crash and Nuke who have big personalities, but who use those personalities to help the tribe achieve its mission in the outside world rather than cause friction inside the tribe. As a chieftain your job is to match good people with expert skills and the resources they need in positions in which they can advance the tribe's mission. Then get out of the way and let them work their magic.

With Crash riding him for several months, Nuke transformed from a selfish, insecure rookie into a dominant pitcher and maturing professional. At a press conference he told the reporters, using the polished nonchalance Crash had taught him, "I'm just happy to be here and I hope I can help the ball club. I just want to give it my best shot, and lord willing, things will work out."

### What Do You Stand For?

"Look at you in those candy-ass monkey suits," said Jake Blues in *The Blues Brothers* movie to his old bandmates, wearing red velvet tuxedos and playing cover tunes at a rundown Holiday Inn. "You were the backbone, the nerve center of a great rhythm-and-blues band. You can make that live, breathe, and jump again." Elwood—Jake's brother—leaned forward to add, "We're on a mission from God."

What do you stand for? A paycheck for trivial, easy work with no larger meaning? Or do you stand for the mission of a living, breathing tribe?

Kōnosuke Matsushita had a profound spiritual experience at a Shinto shrine in 1932. He gathered his team to make an announcement that would guide his company, Matsushita Electric Housewares Manufacturing, for many years to come.

He laid out a bold vision of what his tribe stood for: "The mission of a manufacturer is to overcome poverty by producing an abundant supply of goods. Even though water can be considered a product, no one objects if a passerby drinks from a roadside tap. That is because the supply of water is plentiful, and its price is low. Our mission as a manufacturer is to create material abundance by providing goods as plentifully and inexpensively as tap water. This is how we can banish poverty, bring happiness to people's lives, and make this world a better place."

Matsushita was born in a Japanese farming village in 1894. As a boy he realized electricity was the new wave of the future, and he apprenticed as a teenager at the Osaka Electric Light Company. When he was 22 he became dissatisfied by his job's lack of challenges. He was unfulfilled, and he launched a new company in a decrepit building. He designed a two-way socket that earned his fledgling firm a reputation for high quality at a low price. In those days, electrical products were considered luxury items, so Matsushita turned his attention to making electrical appliances affordable for the average consumer, including items such as lamps, irons, and radios.

Having a mission gives a tribe a skeleton around which to build. But the tribe also needs an identity to put flesh on the bones. A mission gives a tribe the *what* it needs in terms of an objective to pursue. But the tribe's identity also gives it the *why* and *how* it needs to know how to proceed. Knowing what the tribe stands for brings its identity to life.

Well-led tribes are always changing. Successful chieftains don't view their tribes as machines. They view them as living organisms with a heart and a soul. Machines don't stand for anything. They exist to serve a function. But a living, breathing tribe that is cared for, nurtured, and lovingly grown is able to stand for something larger than itself. As chieftain, it is up to you to infuse the tribe with your positive energy and good character. Allow your values to permeate and be absorbed by the tribe so that the members do things the right way even when you are not around.

Over many decades, Matsushita and his tribal members grew their company into one of the largest in the world and accomplished the mission he set in 1932. The company he founded continues to stand for improving people's standard of living through offering high-quality electronic devices at a very low price. It is now known to us as Panasonic. And it has made a vast array of useful electronic devices available in every country in the world at affordable commodity prices.

The Blues Brothers Band, a group "powerful enough to turn goat piss into gasoline," achieved its divine mission too. The band sold out an auditorium, blew the audience's minds, and earned the money needed to save an orphanage—all within the scope of the tribe's mission, which was to *seek a higher calling*. Like Matsushita or the Blues Brothers, you and your tribe won't mind the hard work that comes with executing the tribal mission if there is a purpose larger than the tribe itself embedded within it.

## Someone They Could Trust

"All they needed was someone they could trust to run the casino, and who better than Ace? They wanted him because he ate, slept, and breathed gambling. Ace Rothstein was a hell of a handicapper. He made his first bet when he was 15 years old and he always made money. But he didn't bet like you or me. He bet like a brain surgeon. He had to know everything, this guy. He'd find out the kind of inside stuff nobody else knew, and that's what he put his money on. He'd know if the quarterback was on coke, or if his girlfriend was knocked up. He'd get the wind velocity so he could judge the field goals. He even figured out the different bounce you got off the different kinds of wood on college basketball courts. He was the only guaranteed winner I ever knew."

In the movie *Casino*, East Coast mobsters who can't risk traveling west of Kansas City delegate the operations of an entire Las Vegas casino to Ace Rothstein. And based on his best friend's description, we can understand why they had such profound respect for him.

Chieftains multiply their efforts and train their tribespeople by delegating duties. The tribe can only grow as fast as the chieftain can train or recruit lieutenants and delegate responsibilities to them. This is how chieftains enable themselves to be in several places at once and how tribal members learn to be leaders and increase their own value to the tribe.

- *Avoid the quicksand.* The tribe has myriad objectives to achieve and problems to solve along the mission path. Chieftains who personally handle too many of these will be dragged down into the quicksand. Conserve your energy by allocating objectives and challenges of medium importance to your trusted lieutenants.

- *Responsibility resides with the chieftain.* The chieftain is responsible for the tribe, its members, and moving the tribal mission forward. Even when a task is delegated, final responsibility still belongs to the chieftain. The chieftain must delegate to the right person, monitor their progress, and assist if there are missteps.
- *Distribute your power.* When a chieftain leads with an iron hand, the tribe members will only listen for a while before they start to tune out. Sharing power with other leaders within the tribe and allowing these leaders to confer directly with one another gives the tribe more overall strength.
- *The chieftain's changing role.* When a chieftain forms a new tribe, it is not uncommon to put in 80-hour weeks and treat the tribe like a newborn baby. Over time, as the tribe becomes established, it is difficult to keep up this level of effort. The chieftain must bring in talented people, delegate, and let them help execute the mission.

In the 1960s, Chuck Yeager served as a wing commander in the Vietnam War with five squadrons to oversee. He told his senior officers, "I'm not able to stay on top of everything that's going on under my command, so I have to trust you, my commanders, to set me straight. I'm not a second-guesser, and you can run things your way for as long as you get good results. If I see you making some of the same mistakes I made when I was a squadron commander, I won't hesitate to point them out. Otherwise, you won't find me breathing down your neck. Hell, this is a learning process for me as well."

As a chieftain you are now responsible for "coaching other coaches" and letting them coach the players. In entrusting leaders within the tribe to handle key tasks, the chieftain must ensure they aren't just smart and daring, but are also capable of leading and executing. Don't delegate important tasks to tribespeople who have never run anything or who have no track record of being able to solve problems on a scale applicable to the tasks being delegated. And remember, you didn't bring all these team members into your tribe just so you could do all the work yourself.

## Scarcity = Conflict

"People were counting me out after twenty-five years of being number one," Oprah Winfrey told *People* in 2013. She had suffered the symptoms of a nervous breakdown. The Oprah Winfrey Network she founded had a rough start in 2011 and continued to struggle for ratings. Specialized niche cable channels were in their infancy, and Oprah's network had to be propped up with a $509 million loan. Paying viewers were a scarce resource. There just weren't enough customers willing to pay to watch Oprah's cable programming when they had been accustomed to watching her on free network TV.

There are three primary conditions that flow through and deeply affect all people's experience of life on Earth:

- *Scarce resources* such as land, energy, timber, minerals, food, and water are available in limited quantities.
- *Sharing is a learned behavior.* The scarcer, and therefore the more valuable, a resource is, the less willing people are to share.
- *Scarcity can lead to conflict.* Conflicts result when sharing mechanisms, such as negotiations and markets, break down.

In today's world, customers are also a scarce resource. In ancient times, land and the things that could be extracted or grown from it, were the primary resources. A few thousand years ago, the Roman people were constantly running out of land for farming. Rome, which began as a small settlement along the Tiber River in 753 BC, steadily expanded over time. First into a city, then into a nation, and finally into an empire over a thousand-year span. Rome sustained itself by using its institutionalized and highly effective military to conquer new lands and their inhabitants. It eventually encompassed 90 million people. Rome also transitioned from allied tribes to a monarchy to a democratic republic to a military dictatorship before collapsing under its own weight.

Conflict, like that between eternally expanding ancient Rome and its neighboring peoples, nearly always has its roots in the *scarcity of resources*. Any attempt to live in harmony with others and with the world at large must begin by considering that resources required by people and tribes and other groups are limited in quantity and availability. Scarcity of these resources makes them valuable. As pointed out by Panasonic founder, Kōnosuke Matsushita, if a resource is plentiful, like water in Japan, then sharing is easy. But when it comes to scarce resources the opposite holds true.

Religion and philosophy have at their core a goal of eliminating conflict by altering resource imbalances. Communism seeks to equalize resources via governmental distribution. Buddhism seeks to decrease the need for resources by rejecting desire. Christianity seeks to delay enjoyment of resources until reaching a realm of plenty in the afterlife. And capitalism seeks to allocate resources through markets. Despite noble motives, the elimination of conflict from the world will be difficult to achieve as long as mankind is confined to Earth and resources remain limited in quantity. As a result, a core role of leaders throughout history has been to efficiently utilize the scarce resources they control and work to expand those resources.

Within a few years of her near–nervous breakdown in 2013, Oprah's fortunes rebounded. She and her team added more programming to win viewers. Their timing was good as overall cable viewership increased as Oprah had predicted. She parlayed her network into a $2.5 billion net worth.

Tribes never remain constant in size. Just as in nature with animals and plants, whatever does not expand will inevitably contract. The role of the chieftain is to utilize existing tribal resources to compete with other groups for resources, which allows the tribe to prosper and expand. A chieftain must assume that scarcity will lead to conflicts with competing groups.

## Questing for Resources

"Magellan was rapidly weakening from the effects of the poisoned arrow in his leg, wrote Laurence Bergreen in *Over the Edge of the World*. "In the course of the voyage, Magellan had outwitted death many times. He overcame natural hazards ranging from storms to scurvy, and human hazards in the form of mutinies." But now the Cebuans, in what is today the Philippines, fell upon him in the surf with scimitars and bamboo spears.

It was arguably the most important maritime voyage ever undertaken. Perhaps even riskier and far-flung than the voyage to the moon four hundred years later. Ferdinand Magellan and his crew had been on the ultimate quest for scarce resources, the fabled Spice Islands of the Moluccas, as Bergreen described: "Volcanic ash enriched the soil on the islands where the spices grew, and the moist climate also promoted lush growth; this combination made them unique for spices."

Magellan and more than half of his men perished, and only one of his four ships returned to Spain from the 60,000-mile journey and first complete circumnavigation of the Earth. Spices were so valuable to Europeans in the 1500s that the 50 tons of cloves the expedition returned with still turned a profit for Magellan's backers.

In ancient times, well before Magellan's journey, life was short. A person might not expect to live beyond the age of 40, and there was no retirement or old age as we know it today. In prehistoric tribal times it was very difficult to accumulate resources or wealth, because all work was done with human or animal power, there were no machines or vehicles, food could not be preserved, and people lived a seminomadic life following herds of game animals and didn't want to own heavy or bulky items. In these hunter-gatherer times people spent their entire lives questing for resources in order to feed and clothe themselves, consuming resources shortly after obtaining them.

By 2000 BC there were towns with buildings, clothes made of fabric, widespread agriculture, and jewelry and coins made of precious metals. In these times rulers could extract a surplus from the people they ruled and began to accumulate resources and wealth in the permanent settlements in which they lived.

During this era—according to the Bible—Moses led his people to Mount Sinai, and on to the Canaan border. From there he sent in scouts, who returned with samples of the Promised Land's abundant resources such as huge bunches of grapes that required two men to carry them suspended from a pole. They were elated that Canaan was "overflowing with milk and honey"' but also warned that the Promised Land was inhabited by giants.

One of the primary givens of life is that if a tribe or other group possesses or builds something valuable, others will attempt to replicate or take it. Tribes need to grow in order to accomplish their mission, and this growth is funded or fed by competing with other groups for scarce resources. People, as a rule, do not wish to share desirable resources they possess or control. So in order to obtain the resources needed by the tribe, a chieftain must impose the tribe's will. Moses would either have to:

- Impose his will by force, or
- Impose his will by diplomacy and negotiations.

When a tribe is pursuing its mission and growing by questing for resources, there is a feeling as the tribe matches up against larger and more established competitors, such as the giants of Canaan, that "we're all in this together." This feeling of group pride, unity, and *esprit de corps* is very powerful. And it is very important that a chieftain not allow it to fade. Whatever is not expanding is contracting, and so it is always the Chieftain's ultimate responsibility to keep the momentum of the tribal mission growing.

## Neutralize Competitors

According to a 2011 *Forbes* article, Steve Jobs paid Bill Gates a "weird seduction visit" in the early 1980s, showing off his idea for a cool new technology while emphasizing how much he didn't need Gates's help. But Gates not only didn't fall for Jobs's pitch, he used his great listening skills to gain the upper hand.

Jobs had flown up to Seattle to sell Gates on having Microsoft develop software for the new Apple Macintosh computer. He believed the Macintosh's groundbreaking graphic interface would revolutionize personal computers. Gates agreed to assist, and for several years the joint effort seemed to be going as planned. But then Gates pulled the rug out from under Jobs. In 1985 Gates's Microsoft brought to market its new Windows software, with a more advanced graphic interface than the Macintosh system. Gates had recognized from the start the enormous potential of computers featuring graphic interfaces with visual icons. And he couldn't allow Apple to pull ahead of Microsoft in this revolutionary new area.

When we discuss conflicts between tribes, particularly in a business setting, there is a tendency to use military and sports metaphors. Words such as *conquering*, *defeating*, and *winning* are applicable in wars and athletic competitions in which one side is the clear winner. But for the vast majority of chieftains and their tribes, these metaphors are insufficient to describe ongoing competition with other tribes or groups.

It is much more useful to think in terms of *neutralizing* opponents rather than defeating or destroying them. Tribes engaged in the same field of endeavor, like early Apple and early Microsoft, are constantly competing with one another. Harmony among tribes is not the natural state. On the contrary, competition, maneuvering, and even deception is the norm. In the pursuit of executing the tribal mission via questing for scarce resources, friction between tribes is not unusual.

However, it is better to outthink and outmaneuver the tribe's competitors than to engage in a larger, sustained and potentially costly confrontation if possible. When frictions escalate, entering into negotiation and diplomacy in an effort to avoid outright confrontation is usually the preferred path. The chieftain enters every negotiation clearly understanding how their tribe's strengths and weaknesses match up against the other tribe's. The chieftain has thought through the other tribe's resources, needs, likely offers, responses, and postures. The chieftain's goal in negotiations is to offer several carefully structured alternatives to the other party, any of which will achieve the tribe's objectives.

*Negotiation* is based on using the truth to create a position of strength—presenting the most favorable facts in the best possible light—in order to persuade a competitor. *Confrontation* is based on deception and manipulation—bluffing and posturing to affect an adversary's behavior in the search for an area of weakness—and acting with force if necessary.

Never telegraph your punches. A wise chieftain seeks to determine the competitor's plan and learn where they are strong and vulnerable before moving decisively either via negotiation or confrontation at an opportune moment. To be a good chieftain to your people, or parent to your children, requires predictability. Negotiation and confrontation, however, may require being predictable punctuated by being unpredictable.

Steve Jobs was ousted from Apple in 1985, which led to severe contraction of revenues and momentum at the company. In the late 1990s, when Apple's board decided to bring Jobs back, Gates found a way to neutralize Apple again. This time he did it under the guise of having Microsoft provide Apple a financial lifeline, which created an ongoing armistice between the two firms. When Jobs died in 2011, Gates praised him by saying they "spurred each other on, even as competitors."

## Building an Alliance

"Now you will see what it is like to pedal the bicycle," said Maurizio Gucci, explaining about how hard it is for a chieftain to push forward at all times without the tribe taking a spill. He had been ousted, and longtime company officer Domenico De Sole became CEO. "It was difficult for family-owned firms such as Gucci to attract and control capital and professional management resources they desperately needed to stay in the race," said Maurizio.

When Gucci's revenues declined in 1997 due to a recession in Asia, Bernard Arnault, the billionaire founder of luxury goods group LVMH (which owns Louis Vuitton, Moët & Chandon, and Hermès among others) decided to launch a hostile takeover. Critics called him "The Wolf in Cashmere." By 1999 Arnault had accumulated a 34 percent stake in Gucci. Though alarmed and perturbed, De Sole was just as much a fighter as Arnault. As Sara Forden wrote in *House of Gucci*, "Over the years he had transformed himself from a subservient, awkward, and badly dressed lieutenant into a commanding, articulate CEO" featured on the cover of *Forbes* as a "brand builder."

De Sole searched for a white knight. And he found François Pinault, one of France's richest men. Pinault had transformed a family sawmill into Europe's largest retail group, Printemps. De Sole told Pinault of his dream of turning Gucci into a multi-brand company, and a Gucci-Pinault alliance was formed. Through this alliance, De Sole wrested Gucci away from Arnault. And Pinault gave Gucci the famed Yves Saint Laurent design house to run, a business that Arnault wanted to purchase but couldn't operate on his own. Gucci would become a multi-brand luxury goods group like LVMH, and complete its transformation from tribe to institution.

The natural tendency of tribes is to compete with one another for resources needed to carry out the tribal mission and expand, unless:

- A chieftain like Steve Jobs seeks to build an alliance with a chieftain like Bill Gates to obtain specialized help for an important project.
- Some large external threat, like the "The Wolf in Cashmere," forces a tribe like Gucci to build an alliance in order to survive.

Ultimately, most tribes will at some point need to ally with another tribe or larger group. A significant tribal mission can't be accomplished without eventually needing specialized help from outside the tribe. And the longer a tribe is in existence the greater the odds become that it will need to join forces with other tribes to neutralize or defeat an existential threat from a larger and more powerful tribe or institution.

It is imperative to learn how to cooperate with other tribes when your objectives overlap and your tribe lacks the resources needed to go it alone. The alliance with Pinault is an excellent example of a "1+1=3" alliance. It helped Gucci defend itself from a takeover, but it was also an offensive opportunity, as Gucci gained control of Yves Saint Laurent.

One person can't build a house; it takes a lot of people and money coming together over a period of time to build even a modest home. The same is true of carrying out a substantial and important tribal mission and surviving as a tribe. The chieftain will need at times to call on the assistance and resources of other tribes.

Before entering into any alliance with other groups, make certain you understand their resources, their incentives, and their goals very clearly. You don't want to end up in a situation like Steve Jobs in which your ally, Bill Gates, agrees to help you but becomes an even more direct competitor and larger threat by borrowing your ideas. And be sure to retain the power to untangle the alliance when you choose. As long as your unique tribal mission remains intact, you can consider forging alliances with other tribes. You can rejoice when tribes in your alliance accomplish their goals. Help other tribes, and allow other tribes to help yours.

## Difficult Decisions

"I borrowed $85 million and bought *Martha Stewart Living* [magazine] from Time Warner," said Martha Stewart of her most difficult business decision. Her friends and advisors questioned her: "Why would people buy the magazine when they could watch me on television for free?"

But Stewart was undaunted. "My vision was broader than simply controlling my magazine. The purchase would provide a platform from which the company could grow in many different directions." She executed her strategy by adding television, radio, books, and newspaper columns, and the value soared. Within two years Stewart paid off her debts, and the former model, stockbroker, and caterer became a billionaire.

Decision-making is the fabric of life. Every person and chieftain makes decisions all day long, every day. Sleep in late or wake up early? Put in extra time working on a tribe project on a Sunday or spend time at home with the family? However, the term "difficult decision" as used in these pages refers to a significant, complex, and multifaceted choice a chieftain must make that can affect the tribe and its mission fundamentally for years to come. Making decisions involving substantial risks, trade-offs, and time are among the most important and difficult things a chieftain must do.

At the start of the novel *Jurassic Park*, a mad scientist entrepreneur, John Hammond, has chosen to clone dinosaurs to populate his theme park and thereby earn a fortune. We infer that due to his dogged optimism and avarice, this decision was an easy one for Hammond to make.

That scenario makes a terrific plot for a science-fiction book and a thrilling action movie. But if dinosaur-cloning were reality rather than fiction, would it really be such an easy decision? If you were the chieftain of a theme park, and your tribe had developed the ability to clone a Tyrannosaurs Rex and make billions of dollars, would you use it? Would you bring a 40-foot-long killing machine with foot-long dagger-like teeth back to life?

You could sculpt your decision by evaluating the following factors:

- *Is what you are considering unethical?* Decide not to proceed if it is.
- *Identify all options.* Eliminate options with large downside risks that can't be controlled. Find ways to reduce risks in remaining options.
- Can you turn your best option into *a series of small decisions* so that you can procure more time and course-correct along the way?
- Give yourself a *decision deadline.* The only thing worse than making the wrong decision is having to alter course without any time left.
- Sometimes it is best to delay your decision. *Let circumstances clarify.* Allow risks to resolve themselves.

Conrad Hilton wrote in *Be My Guest* that he learned through his coursework at the New Mexico School of Mines how to reduce problems into their simplest and clearest form. And he used this skill frequently in his decision-making: "I was to be faced with large financial problems—enormous business deals with as many ramifications as an octopus has arms—where bankers, lawyers, consultants, all threw in their particular bit of information. It is always necessary to listen carefully to the powwow, but in the end, someone has to put them all together, see the actual problem for what it is, and make a decision [to] come up with the answer."

Being highly intelligent isn't the same as being a good decision-maker. And a lot of spectacular failures weren't the result of a single bad decision, but rather were produced by a series of small decisions that amplified one another. The future will always be an unknown, so a chieftain must use the best information and analysis available combined with instincts honed over time, and confidently move the tribe forward.

## Tribes vs. Institutions

Teams of woolly mammoths strained as they dragged massive limestone blocks to the pyramid construction site, as depicted in the 2008 film *10,000 BC*. Foremen barked orders to thousands of stoneworkers to keep them on task. From within a lavish silk tent, an almighty ruler adorned with gold grumbled to his lieutenants, "They must work faster!"

People often think of leadership in fanciful, idealized terms—a pharaoh building pyramids, a general commanding vast platoons of soldiers, or a car-company CEO watching millions of vehicles roll out of a factory. But in the grand sweep of history, very few leaders will ever occupy one of these supreme leadership positions in a highly centralized and hierarchal organization. The most common form of leadership is, and probably always will be, more similar to that of the tribal chieftain, who must earn the trust of the tribe through charisma and character, and by recruiting and motivating tribal members through laying out a compelling tribal mission.

USC Film School graduate George Lucas set up his own tribe by founding Lucasfilm Ltd. in 1973, and making the low-budget but critically acclaimed *American Graffiti*. He then went on to create two of the most financially successful and beloved movie franchises of all time, the Star Wars and Indiana Jones films. In the 1980s Lucas added an audio company, a visual-effects company, and a gaming company, effectively completing the transformation of Lucasfilm from a tribe into an institution. Having lost much of his fortune in a divorce, in the 1990s and early 2000s Lucas produced new Star Wars and Indiana Jones films. Though these movies were financially successful, they were considered by both fans and critics to be formulaic and lacking the originality and emotion of the originals. In 2012 Lucas announced he was retiring from making Hollywood blockbuster films and going back to making smaller independent films, a return to his original mission. And he sold Lucasfilm to the Walt Disney Company for $4 billion.

Lucas had grown his tribe into an institution over a period of several decades. So did Phil Knight with Nike. And Kōnosuke Matsushita with Panasonic. And Steve Jobs with Apple. To generalize for the purpose of these pages, a *tribe* is a group of between 30 and 100 individuals. An *institution* is a group that at one point was a tribe, but has now grown to a size such that not all the members are able to know one another. As a rule, tribes tend to only grow to a certain size before either breaking apart into several tribes, growing into an institution, or being acquired or absorbed by an institution.

- *Tribes focus on* belonging, solidarity, relationships, flexibility, agility, values, and customs. They feature a relatively small amount of specialization among their members, and their chieftains and other leaders obtain their power through consensus.
- *Institutions focus on* power, hierarchy, control, deliberateness, rules, and bureaucracies. They are effective at coordinating large and complex endeavors such as major construction projects, military campaigns, and high-volume manufacturing.

Tribes have missions, as do individuals. Institutions and other large organizations have ideologies and agendas. Tribes exist to carry out the tribal mission—developed and overseen by the chieftain—and to provide for the tribespeople. Members of institutions are expected to promote the well-being of the institution itself. Institutions have both producers and allocators of resources, but within tribes essentially all members are producers.

However, institutions have more total resources and tend to be more stable than tribes, so many people who one day want to build a tribe begin at an institution to gain experience. Tribes have many advantages as vehicles for executing a mission, but they typically aren't as effective for carrying out large, complex, geographically dispersed, or multifaceted endeavors. Leaders should carefully consider the differences between executing a mission versus building pyramids.

## A Powerful Tribe

What sports "tribe" won 10 national championships in a 12-year period? And how could such a feat of greatness have been accomplished? Was it through having a bigger payroll than their opponents? Or, was it through having an unparalleled coach-player duo that stayed together for twenty years? No, it wasn't the New York Yankees or the New England Patriots. In fact, all of this team's players were unpaid volunteers, and none played for the team for longer than four years.

Yes, it was the UCLA Bruins men's basketball team, coached by their chieftain, the Wizard of Westwood, John Wooden. In 1948 he took over an underperforming program in a cramped gym, and turned it into a national powerhouse with 10 NCAA championships. It was the greatest turnaround in sports history. Paradoxically, his success was derived not from trying to win championships, but by a mission of molding young men into people of character. Players believed in Wooden and in his program and wanted to play for the Bruins, so he was able to replenish his tribe as his student-athletes graduated.

His coaching philosophy was simple, yet ahead of its time. He believed in outworking the other teams at Bruins' practices, and in having the team play games as a selfless unit rather than as a collection of self-centered star players. Above all, what led the Bruins to greatness was not a philosophy of winning at all costs but rather a philosophy of seeking tribal greatness: "Success is peace of mind," Wooden said, "which is a direct result of self-satisfaction in knowing you did your best to become the best that you are capable of becoming." In other words, the pursuit not of happiness via winning, but of broader and further-reaching fulfillment.

Like John Wooden, guide your tribe to greatness:

- *Accomplish the impossible.* As a chieftain it is your job to put a compelling and important mission before your people, not an easy one. When they tell you that you are asking the impossible, say: "You're right, it probably is impossible. But if it could be done, how would we do it?"

- *Greatness, not perfection.* In the history of the world there has never been a tribe made up of all perfect people. As chieftain it is up to you to show your people how to work together to overcome each other's weaknesses. Your objective is to lead the tribe to greatness, not to perfection.

- *Be flexible and adaptable.* The greatness of the tribe will be accomplished by the greatness of your leadership. Hold true to the essence of your personal code, but be flexible in your leadership as the situation requires. You will lead your people through many challenges, each requiring a different solution. Be adaptable.

- *Begin anew tomorrow.* Success is never final—there's always more to be done in executing the mission. Celebrate your successes and milestones, but then begin anew with hunger and desire for the next achievement along the mission path. Make certain you don't allow the tribe to be wrecked by success.

When your time as chieftain is done, hopefully your people will be proud to have served with you in achieving the tribe's mission. Hopefully the execution of the mission will have made a positive impact in people's lives. Hopefully your trusted lieutenants will be ready to lead their own tribes. And hopefully, as you move on to the legacy stage of life, both your tribe's allies and competitors will be compelled to say:

*"They were a powerful tribe. No challenge was too great for them to overcome. No force could stop them. They set an enormous mission for themselves and made the world better by achieving it. When they put their minds to something, they accomplished anything they wanted."*

# 5. LEAVE LEGACY

**Legacy Replaces Mission**

He was both the youngest and oldest surfer ever to win a world championship. Since turning pro in 1990, Kelly Slater has won 11 World Surf League championships through competing in events at the best surf spots all around the globe, including Hawaii, Tahiti, Australia, Brazil, South Africa, Japan, France, and California. And he has bested professionals in competitive events who had not even been born yet when he won his first world title. Few athletes have come close to the level of Slater's sustained success over the course of his professional career. He is the ultimate competitor, and arguably the greatest professional athlete of all time.

In addition to these championships and career successes and the respect of his peers, Slater has also appeared in movies, authored books, and has made tens of millions of dollars in prize winnings, sponsorships, and through his entrepreneurial endeavors including his surfboard and clothing lines. Surprisingly, though, at the zenith of his career, when onlookers would likely have believed he was on top of the world, Slater said: "My competitiveness enabled me to accomplish all my goals. But I realized, after I accomplished them, that my competitiveness was an obstacle, preventing me from being happy." He was still seeking fulfillment.

As you learned during the mission stage of life, the pursuit of your mission is something akin to a necessary addiction or a psychosis you deliberately chose for yourself in your youth. After achieving your mission, you should step away from this addiction when you are able. Often a person who has achieved their mission, or who has achieved their mission many times over in the case of someone like Kelly Slater, seems to be unable to move beyond the compulsive resource-questing behavior that goes with it. This is often due to a subconscious desire to put off having to face the prospect of physical decline and eventual death. The solution to this dilemma is to allow your mission to transition into and be replaced by your legacy.

The legacy stage is the final and most important of the five life stages you must pass through and complete. Your mission is the project you spent your life achieving, and your legacy is what you then go on to leave behind for others. Your legacy lives on even after your death.

For example, now in her 80s, Dr. Jane Goodall no longer tramps around the African bush at dawn with her notebooks. Her mission to personally study primate behavior in the wild has been replaced by her legacy, promoting the Jane Goodall Institute for Wildlife Research, a nonprofit corporation. You, too, must allow legacy to replace mission.

- *More accumulation won't bring fulfillment.* Once you have achieved your mission and accumulated the accolades and wealth that goes with it, more resources, consumption, and toys won't bring you additional fulfillment.

- *Put your energy into something bigger than yourself.* After the mission has been accomplished, you've won. Rather than putting more resources into yourself, the only path to further fulfillment is to put your energy into some larger cause that will outlive you.

- *A pile of gold is a poor chair.* You had the time of your life accumulating prestige, power, and resources. But now, sitting on a pile of gold in your old age won't bring satisfaction. This wealth must be used thoughtfully to benefit others who will live on after you.

Your mission has been achieved. Nothing can erase that. Not even your aging, your physical decline, or your death. At the end of the world, your accomplishments will still be there. That stage of your life is complete, and it is time to move beyond. So clear your mind. Stop struggling and competing and trying to accumulate more of anything. Empty yourself. Let your thoughts drift. Allow your legacy to come into focus.

## Recluses & Oddballs

"There is no one I can't buy," said Howard Hughes, the richest man in the world. But sadly, with no spouse or children, and no close friends or family members, he became ridiculed for his eccentric behaviors. Rather than wielding power, he became a prisoner of his own phobias and neuroses.

At 21, Hughes inherited the Hughes Tool Company from his father and a vast fortune. He moved to Hollywood and plowed his energy and family wealth into motion pictures and aviation. His first film, *Hells Angels*, received an Academy Award for cinematography, and he later purchased RKO Studios. He set the world air-speed record in an airplane he developed, and set another record for the fastest flight around the world. He formed Hughes Aircraft Company, which manufactured the largest airplane ever built, and he purchased Trans World Airlines.

Throughout his life Hughes had a severe phobia of germs and avoided contact with other people as much as possible. After several concussions from aviation injuries, his behavior became increasingly erratic. He lived in a screening room for four months, eating only chocolate bars and chicken. Surrounded by aides and employees who benefited from controlling him, he had no family or friends in his life to question his choices, stage an intervention, or help him get back on track. He went on to buy up most of the large casinos in Las Vegas and spent the rest of his life living in hotels, addicted to codeine and other painkillers. It was a prison with golden bars. He died from kidney failure in 1976 while on a private jet midair between Acapulco and Los Angeles, emaciated and unrecognizable with long hair and fingernails. With a net worth of over $2 billion, he was the richest man in the world, yet had no descendants and left no viable will.

As you determine how to go about building and preserving your legacy, consider that much of history and human progress is the story of recluses, inheritors of vast resources, childless specializers, and oddballs:

- *People like Hughes and Alexander*, who inherited institutions their fathers built, and amassed the world's largest fortunes of their times, but died surrounded by their officers, with no children or will.

- *People like Confucius and Buddha*, who each lost a parent while young, yet abandoned their own families during their time of developing and promoting their groundbreaking life philosophies.

- *People like Napoleon and Hitler*, who each felt belittled while young, and put all their energy into revenge and conquest, leading their countries to war and causing death for millions of innocents.

The history of the world has been made by a small number of people. By a handful of kings, inventors, conquerors, philosophers, generals, politicians, scientists, and writers. We owe thanks to many of them for improvements they have made to the lives of all the people who came after them. And yet, a great many of them were not the kind of people that you would want to meet for a drink or spend any amount of time around. Nor would you want to loan them money, live next door to them, or let them date your sister. Many of them were incredibly driven but downright odd.

Theirs isn't the life you would want for yourself or your children, because they went through it not thinking or caring enough about other people. They may have had huge missions, but they didn't live fulfilling lives, because they put their own desires above the needs of others in their orbit. Hopefully you have passed through the first four life stages making good comrades, building a life with a partner you love, investing your time in the next generation, and recruiting and training your tribespeople. Hopefully you have already made a difference and been a positive force in the lives of other people. But if you feel you've spent more of your time than you should have collecting and consuming, you still have the opportunity—right now—through your legacy to be valuable to others.

## Full Trophy Cases

Oprah Winfrey's style as an entrepreneur broadcaster has been so unique that: *The Wall Street Journal* created the term *Oprahfication* to denote her peculiar type of public confession as a vehicle for therapy. *Time*, which described her style as "rapport talk" instead of "report talk," wrote, "She makes people care because she cares. That is Winfrey's genius and will be her legacy.'" Winfrey is the only person ever to have appeared on *Time*'s list of most influential people 10 different times. In our modern society, an implicit goal in nearly any field is "to get to the top," like Winfrey.

Ted Turner made it to the top too. After his father's suicide, 24-year-old Turner inherited his billboard company. As its new chieftain, Turner began diversifying by buying up poorly performing regional radio and television stations to form a broadcasting conglomerate. He purchased the Atlanta Braves and MGM Studios for content, creating an institution he christened Turner Broadcasting. He launched CNN, the world's first 24-hour cable news network to create a global broadcasting platform.

Within several decades, Turner merged his company with Time Warner in a stock deal that made him a multibillionaire. Along the way he also won the America's Cup as a yachtsman, the World Series as an MLB owner, married actress Jane Fonda, and became the largest land owner in the United States. In 1997 he shocked the world by pledging $1 billion to the United Nations and ignited a wave of outsized philanthropy by other American billionaires. He asked, "What good is wealth sitting in the bank?"

In looking more closely at the careers of Hughes, Slater, Winfrey, Turner and others, here are some common refrains from the top:

- *Not so satisfying up there*. It can be a lot more satisfying working one's way up to the top of the mountain than it is trying to remain there. Everyone thinks they want to get to the top, but it can be lonely up there. And many of the people climbing up after you want to knock you off. The long years of pushing boulders uphill, and the stress and fighting that goes with continuously competing for resources can ultimately drain away all the enjoyment.

- *Full trophy cases and bank accounts*. In the lean early years every small victory and dollar meant something, because you were a swashbuckler and living hand-to-mouth. Once you reach the top, additional awards for your trophy case and money flowing into already-full bank accounts take on a different meaning by becoming more symbolic. These indicators of the world's approval become background noise.

- *Comparisons become pointless*. The urge to compete with others continues to diminish the older you become. In ancient times someone truly could be the tribe's best hunter. But now that there are eight billion human beings inhabiting our planet, it has become nearly impossible to be "the best" at anything. And in any case, you aren't competing with others to be the best chieftain or best parent. Your journey through these roles is unique to you.

Now that you have completed your years as a chieftain, and you have fewer years ahead than behind you, the questions begin to change. Instead of asking, "Am I the best ever?" a person is more inclined to ask, "Did I do everything I wanted to do with everyone I wanted to do it with?"

Warren Buffett the builder of fabled investment firm, Berkshire Hathaway, was inspired by Turner's pledge and committed to donating most of his fortune to the Gates Foundation. Throughout his decades in the public eye, Buffett has consistently resisted using net worth to measure whether a person has reached the top or as a scorecard of personal success. He said, "You are a success if you reach the age of 65, or so, and are loved by all the people you'd like to be loved by. Many rich and famous people are not."

## Passing the Torch

Suffering from "occupational burnout," Dick Vermeil, then-head coach of the Philadelphia Eagles retired from coaching in 1983 a few seasons after losing the Super Bowl to the Oakland Raiders. He appeared to have moved on completely, and spent 15 years working as a football broadcaster. And then, somehow, the St. Louis Rams convinced Vermeil to return to coaching. With a dismal record of 10-22 over his first two seasons as the Rams' new head coach it looked as though he had made the mistake of his life and things couldn't get worse. But they could. In 1999 Vermeil's starting quarterback was injured during the preseason. With no other option he made unknown rookie quarterback Kurt Warner his starter.

Amazingly, the Rams offense exploded. Warner led the NFL in touchdown passes, and "mad scientist" offensive coordinator Mike Martz helped Vermeil create an offense that scored more points than any other that season. They compiled a 13-3 record, won the Super Bowl with a fourth-quarter comeback, and Vermeil was named NFL coach of the year. Vermeil's mission had finally been completed. He had coached his tribe to a championship... And then he passed the torch.

Immediately after the win, with confetti raining down, Vermeil hugged Warner—the NFL MVP and Super Bowl MVP—and told him "I love you." It seemed an unusually raw display of emotion captured in a professional sports broadcast. But when Vermeil announced his retirement again from coaching shortly thereafter, it all made sense. He was passing the torch to Warner—and to Martz, who became his successor as head coach. And the duo led the Rams to several more thrilling seasons as "The Greatest Show on Turf" and another Super Bowl appearance.

The final completion of the tribal mission, old age, or death will eventually remove even the most tenured and greatest chieftains from office. Vermeil hadn't completed his mission when he retired as the Eagles coach, and in hindsight it wasn't his time to move on. But fortunately, the universe provided him another opportunity to complete the mission. When he finally led the Rams tribe to a Super Bowl win 17 years later, he knew the time was finally right to pass the torch. In Martz and Warner he had two worthy lieutenants to whom he could hand off the tribe and know it would continue to be successful.

The wise chieftain has to know when it is the right time to relinquish command of the tribe. They must make preparations in advance for the eventual moment when their time as leader has been completed. This is the final task of the chieftain in ensuring the continuity of the tribe and of caring for their people. Vermeil's emotional embrace of Warner, which was televised to many hundreds of millions of people worldwide in the moments after the Rams' tribal mission had been completed, was both joyous and sad. It was as if Vermeil was telling Warner: *I am handing you the torch, and I will no longer be here every day to remain vigilant to ensure that its fire continues to burn, but that is okay, because I have showed you and the rest of the tribe how to do it, and I have full and complete confidence that you will keep this torch lit.*

Your time as tribal chieftain isn't supposed to last forever. You only receive a finite time in which to lead the tribe forward in the accomplishment of its mission and your own. You must let the tribe and your people go before you overstay your welcome.

Nothing is more touching than for the chieftain to honor those who helped him move mountains as Vermeil did in embracing Warner. Nor is there anything more noble than for a trusted lieutenant to show their deep respect and caring for their chieftain in his moment of passing the torch than Warner did when he returned Vermeil's embrace and said, "I love you too." Everyone watching could see and feel Vermeil's sentiment: *I've had a great run as chieftain, working alongside the best people in the world, and I have no regrets.*

## Five Forms of Legacy

"I have nothing to offer but blood, toil, tears and sweat. We have before us many, many long months of struggle and suffering. You ask, what is our policy?... To wage war against a monstrous tyranny, never surpassed in the dark, lamentable catalogue of human crime... What is our aim?... Victory, victory at all costs..." said Winston Churchill, the "British Bulldog," in his first speech as prime minister in 1940. Churchill is known to most people today as the hero who tirelessly promoted democracy, refused to give in to the Nazi regime during World War II, and led the allied forces to victory.

After completing the mission of winning the war, Churchill retired from politics and devoted himself to preserving his legacy through writing. He was a prolific writer throughout his life, and one of his critics jokingly referred to Churchill's *The World Crisis*: "Winston's brilliant autobiography, disguised as the history of the universe." Nonetheless, he won the Nobel Prize for Literature in 1953 for his exhaustive six-volume history of World War II, which cemented his legacy as the greatest leader, statesman, and orator of the 20th century.

The legacy is difficult to define. It is carried out in many different ways and is highly individualized and unique to each person. But all forms of legacy serve as an enduring contribution that a person expects will live on after their death. In this way, all forms of legacy are an attempt at immortality. As described in a previous section, Ernest Becker postulated that the only way to avoid debilitating neurosis resulting from the knowledge that death awaits us is to create an "immortality project" for oneself that will live on after we die. This allows us to 'cheat death.' Think of the completion of the mission as a person's cake, and legacy is the icing on the cake that preserves and cements it for posterity. This allows a person to escape neurosis or depression as they age and the physical body begins to decline significantly in vigor.

Five common forms of legacy are:

- Leaving a family fortune or other inheritance to descendants, and making multigenerational provisions surrounding this gift.
- Philanthropic or other charitable work for an organization or a cause about which a person cares deeply.
- Codifying and expanding the details, facts, and legend of a person's mission, usually by documenting it in writing.
- Leaving control of a platform built around valuable resources, such as a piece of land or a business, to a family member or a lieutenant.
- Assisting young tribal members or chieftains through guidance and mentorship, or through financial support.

In contrast to Turner and Churchill, Coco Chanel had no children. She passed away like Hughes without making definitive plans to preserve her legacy. "Chanel had never groomed a successor," wrote Rhonda Garelick in *Mademoiselle*. She disliked sharing credit with the many talented people who worked for her, and so at the end of her career, no one stood ready to assume responsibility for the house [the Chanel brand]." She worked until the end and passed away in her sleep at 87. Her home was pilfered of her prized jewelry, and "Chanel left almost no directions for her executors." Her vast wealth went to her foundation with no clear mandate for how to use it.

Don't neglect to ice the cake. Don't make it your goal to "retire and play golf." Ensure that you step aside from the mission stage at the appropriate time. And for the sake of both your own state of mind as you age and for the benefit of those you love who will live on after you, be certain to put in the effort to pass through and perform the legacy stage as well as you did the other life stages.

## Wisdom of the Elders

"If he steals our harvest again, we might as well cut our throats and be done with it," said one villager to another in the classic Western *The Magnificent Seven*. Calvera and his band of cutthroat cowboys had ridden in on horseback again with their guns and stolen much of the villagers' crops and food, as they did every year. The villagers, a tribe of peaceful farmers in 1800s Mexico, were easily overpowered by Calvera and his gang.

"Leave the valley. That's what we must do," another villager responded.

"We break our backs in the fields and our bellies stay empty. We must do something," said a third villager. "But what?"

Then, a long pause. Finally, the first villager said, "We'll ask the old man. He'll know."

They went out to the periphery of the village, where the old village wiseman lived in a simple wooden hut next to a craggy outcrop of volcanic rock. They sat together at a low wood table with nothing on it. The wiseman's hair and beard were gray, both trimmed neatly. The furrows in his face were deep, but his eyes brightened as he listened to the three younger men.

"Fight," said the wiseman, "You must fight." As if in explanation he took from his pocket a faded pouch. Out of it he pulled a gleaming gold pocket watch on a long chain. With one last loving glance at his most prized possession, he handed it to the men. They would go on to sell the watch for funds to hire the help they needed to rout Calvera and save their village.

In times gone by, an older man who was no longer able to hunt came to find great enjoyment in teaching and advising the boys and young men of the tribe. He helped them to become great hunters. He also shared the stories and legends of the tribe's colorful and illustrious past, using them to teach the younger generations and make them laugh. Having raised his own children to adulthood, the *wiseman* became a father to the tribe.

In times gone by, a mother with adult children helped her daughters, or anyone who needed help, with childbirth and caring for and raising the tribe's children. She was an expert storyteller, but also very good at listening to the problems and fears of the new parents and the young leaders within the tribe. She had learned not to offer advice except when it was requested, but everyone felt better after speaking with her, and hardly a day went by that she did not receive multiple visitors. They called her *grandmother*, but in truth she was a mother to the tribe.

Similarly, Golda Meir, prime minister of Israel, became a grandmother to her people after she retired. She was the first woman to serve as the head of state of a Western nation, a predecessor to Margaret Thatcher and Angela Merkel. In retirement, Meir, like Churchill, published memoirs and became a revered motherly figure. Eleanor Roosevelt said of Meir: "Her interest is human beings, her preoccupation is human beings, and her every thought is for human beings."

In today's modern world it sounds somewhat strange to call a person a wiseman or a grandmother (except a woman's own biological grandchildren), but we can refer to both now as "elders." A tribesperson is responsible for performing work. A chieftain is responsible for influencing others to perform work under his or her supervision. And an elder is responsible for serving as a conduit of knowledge. An elder gives this knowledge to the young and preserves the traditions of the tribe.

Elders no longer bear the brunt of responsibility for production and execution within the tribe. The people who need an elder's knowledge the most are often those who least realize how important elders' accumulated wisdom is to the tribe's ability to prosper.

**Elegant and Unrushed**

"The players are so tall these days the basket should be raised a few feet. And the officials shouldn't let them travel with the ball; they have to dribble more," my dad overheard one senior citizen say to another, sipping coffee at a donut shop. The man doing the listening nodded attentively. Eventually, he leisurely folded up the sports section, and excused himself, "I'm afraid I need to leave now, but I enjoyed hearing all your great suggestions for how basketball could be improved. It was nice meeting you and I hope to see you again. Here's my card." The first man looked down at the card, which simply said JOHN WOODEN. He had no idea he had been airing his thoughts to the Wizard of Westwood!

Yes, John Wooden, the pioneering UCLA basketball coach, was perennially polite, graceful, and known for his elegant demeanor. Like Wooden, everyone at some point has been on the receiving end of a "silver fox" setting the record straight on how things were better back in the day.

And this was probably the reason *Grumpy Old Men*, a comedy starring Walther Matthau and Jack Lemmon, was able to earn $71 million at the box office and solid reviews in 1993. The entire audience is in on the joke when there is not just one, but *two* grumpy old men sharing the screen. And that setup allows them to take out their impatience and finger-wagging know-it-all-ness on each other rather than on any innocent bystanders from the younger generation.

In person, though, grumpy old men aren't as endearing as they are on television or in the movies. In fact, nothing puts a child or new adult to sleep faster than a frail older person talking incessantly about their past, and the glory of their accomplishments, and how things were better in their day. That is why your role as an elder is to speak to young people about *their future* through the prism of your experiences, rather than about *your past*.

During the legacy stage, share your wisdom with the young. Help them avoid depression by encouraging them to pursue adventures, stay on the mission path, nurture their family, build a strong tribe, etc. You haven't lived a perfect life. Nobody has. So yes, you can speak to the young of some of your triumphs, but also be certain to share where you had setbacks and where you were humbled, both in your work and in your relationships.

As a person grows older their inner essence continues to emerge, and they gradually become their true self, because they don't have to put on an act for anyone or try to win favor. Owing to this, some people reach old age as irritable and self-centered. On the other hand, an "elder," as the term is used in these pages, is personable and unassuming. An elder exudes a personal style of timeworn elegance, an unrushed economy of motion, and speech that displays confidence but little ego. Their dress and personal effects reflect timelessness and simple elegance, never an attempt to be fashionable or to impress other people. An elder is comfortable in their role and is not looking at this time to accumulate acclaim or possessions. They do, however, enjoy helping the younger generation in these pursuits.

An elder knows what they stand for and their own beliefs. They are comfortable with themselves. Over the years they have seen every sort of situation that can affect an individual, a family, or the tribe, many times over. Nothing surprises them any longer. They know what to do and how to behave calmly and without calling attention to themselves in any situation.

When an elder speaks with a young person they give that person their full attention. Nothing matters more to them than learning what is important to a young person and assisting them. They are not trying to impose or indoctrinate anyone; they just wish to share what has worked for them. A new adult has good health and optimism but owns few things. A chieftain has a home, family, possessions—but those things in a sense own him or her. An elder reverts to a simpler life of no longer being owned.

## Legacy Provides Immortality

***Esquire* magazine**: *Eastwood is eighty-six now. But if you think he's devolved into that old man on your block who walks around talking to squirrels, you're dead wrong. Eastwood does not stop. Never has. Eastwood is still vital and vibrant, still pushing himself creatively.* "Clint, your father retired when he was sixty and died at sixty-four. Does his death haunt you? Like, 'If I stop working, I will drop'?"

**Clint Eastwood**: "Maybe. A lot of people when they retire, they just expire. It happens to men more than women. Women usually have great interest in the family, because the family's always growing and they're always coming to the rescue."

To retire means to leave one's career. You can *retire* from your job. But you can't retire from having a mission. You can only *complete* your mission and then *move on* to working on your legacy. Eastwood played a cowboy in early television shows and in Italian "Spaghetti Western" films, and played an action hero in blockbuster movies like the Dirty Harry franchise for decades. When he aged and was no longer able to play rough-and-tumble roles, he never "retired" from acting, but rather he went behind the camera to produce and direct movies that focused on larger societal issues than blowing up buildings and defeating criminal masterminds. These statement films he is creating are his legacy.

Retirees who aren't working on their legacies tend to want to talk about the past. On the other hand, those who still maintain a connection to their tribe or are working on their legacy are focused on the future. Groups of retirees who meet every day for coffee or at their country club will talk a lot about what they used to do when they were executives or professionals, and many of them are bored out of their minds. As Warren Buffett has said, "Retirees will spend a week planning for their haircut on Sunday."

When people living in hunter-gatherer societies have been exposed to modern man, they are confused by many aspects of industrial-age thinking. In particular, as they live in the "eternal now," they do not understand why modern city people spend so much time contemplating the past and worrying about the future. In their world, aging and time are not sources of anxiety or fear. Old age, physical decline, and eventual death are all part of the natural progression of life that they see in plants, animals, and in their fellow humans. Elders are admired and respected for the depth of wisdom they have built up through many years of hard knocks.

As an elder's life unfolds, a person at last solves the riddle of how to overcome concern over the relentless physical aging of the body. Physical decline is acceptable if, along with it, progress can be made on building the legacy. By shifting attention from one's own body to the legacy, an elder frees themselves from fear of death. The legacy provides the immortality all people seek. No longer fearing death, and having been a productive member of the tribe for many years, an elder has gained the freedom and earned the right to pursue fulfillment and enjoyment through completing the legacy.

Meryl Streep, Eastwood's co-star in *The Bridges of Madison County*, has the legacy of her 20 Oscar nominations and three wins, which may never be equaled. And she has pledged $1 million to the establishment of the National Women's History Museum. "She wanted to support an institution where women's place in history, relegated to sidebars in textbooks, could be collected, archived, and publicized to showcase incredible stories," wrote Erin Carlson in *Queen Meryl*.

You hear people say, *I'm going to retire and spend time with my family*. But that doesn't work. Yes, you should spend as much time with your family as you can, but that can't be your main focus. Your spouse has his or her own friends and hobbies. Your kids are grown and are busy with their own missions and families. Keep working, and shift your work to your legacy.

## Four Belief Systems

"I remember clearly when the first plane flew over. I thought it was a huge bird. We all ran off and hid. Some jumped in streams or under bushes. Everyone clung to each other and cried in fear. This is the end of us all!"

In 1930 three Australian gold prospectors were the first white people to venture into the interior of New Guinea by airplane. They discovered over a million tribesmen who had no knowledge of the outside world. The prospectors brought a motion picture camera with them and captured the initial meeting. Fifty years later the grainy film was found and turned into the 1983 Academy Award–nominated documentary *First Contact*.

One of the pilots said of this indigenous peoples' first encounter with Europeans and modern technology: "They were all in one long line, and they'd come in with food and sugarcane and stuff like that, to show that they were friendly. They thought we were something a bit more than ordinary human beings." These reels of film—which were painstakingly repaired—are one of the best visual records ever made of two peoples with vastly different belief systems coming into contact with one another for the first time.

Humankind has four basic belief systems:

- *Religion*: Organized spirituality with clergy, special texts, and rituals, teaching how to be a good person and have a pleasant afterlife.
- *Magic*: Wielding superpowers or supernatural knowledge, via secret rituals, to gain advantage over the natural world and other humans.

- *Science*: Endeavoring to explain the natural world by formulating rules and laws that apply universally.
- *Philosophy*: Contemplation, analysis and intellection aimed at answering eternal questions such as *How can I live a good life?*

In tribal societies most religions are regional and polytheistic. The New Guinean tribesmen believed the white prospectors were their dead and therefore "faded" ancestors coming back as gods. Religion is a system of values and norms founded on belief in all-powerful beings. The most widespread religions such as Christianity and Islam grew by worshipping a single deity and through missionary efforts. Modern religions teach that to live is to suffer, and we will be rewarded for being good and enduring.

Magic and science offer competing explanations of the natural world. The indigenous New Guineans thought the airplane was a metal bird powered by magic. The prospectors viewed the plane's power as coming from a combustion engine and wings that produce lift. Phenomena which can't be explained are often attributed to magic. The rules and formulas of science, such as Newton's laws of motion, are viewed as sacredly as religious texts, because they obey external forces that can't be altered by humans.

Philosophy picks up where science leaves off. Science tells us *how* the natural world works, and philosophy tells us *what* humans should do with their lives. The Australian prospectors chose to spend their lives pursuing gold and money. The New Guineans didn't care about gold and didn't know what money was. They judged a man's worth by how many shell necklaces and pigs he owned. Most philosophies are not missionary, but some—like communism, capitalism, nationalism, and Buddhism—are missionary.

There is overlap among these four belief systems, because none offers a total explanation. Humankind has a deep thirst for a system that: 1) explains the natural world through axioms; 2) tells us how to live our lives; and 3) eases our fears about death. It is the elder's role to distill a lifetime of knowledge for the young, share what they have learned, and provide the explanations the younger generations crave.

## A Spiritual Awakening

"I went to the woods because I wished to live deliberately," said author and transcendentalist leader Henry David Thoreau, "to front only the essential facts of life, and see if I could learn what it had to teach, and not, when I came to die, discover that I had not lived. I wanted to live deep and suck out all the marrow of life, to live so sturdily and Spartan-like as to put to rout all that was not life."

Thoreau built a cabin in the woods near Walden Pond in Massachusetts in the 1850s. His goal was to immerse himself in his surroundings, try to be self-sufficient by growing his own vegetables, and have time to write and commune with nature. For over two years he lived there, taking long walks, reflecting on simple living and producing his masterwork, *Walden*, which details his experiences. Among his main themes are that one must pursue spiritual awakening in order to realize the truths of life, because these are often obscured by all the daily errands, chores, socializing, and consumerism composing a busy modern existence.

A spiritual awakening—or soulfulness—isn't necessarily religious or mystical, but it could be. It is *seeing deeply and experiencing appreciation* for what we may call the universe, nature, destiny, karma or God. Soulfulness tends to be brought out in people when they are able to spend long blocks of time totally immersed in doing something and can be alone with their own thoughts without interruption. Those who play team sports will tell you all about the teamwork and discipline they learned through their sport. On the other hand, solo-sport athletes, like surfers, will tend to use many spiritual or even quasi-religious terms to describe ocean conditions, their favorite surf breaks, and even the innate energy of their surfboards.

Ancient agrarian peoples imbued with spiritual descriptions their farmlands, crops, and the interplay of their farming activities with the cycles of the sun and moon and rain. Similarly, modern businesspeople in the finance world will imbue with spiritual or mystical terminology stocks, companies, money, and the interplay of their financial activities with the cycles of the market and the fiscal calendar. A farmer would say that the behavior of financial markets is explainable by cause-and-effect. A businessperson would say the same about the growing of crops. Which is to say that seeing deeply into the nature of things has to be experienced for oneself and cannot be transferred or explained from one person to another.

Drawing out a spiritual awakening through immersion in an activity or in nature often leads to profound humility. In *Last of the Bluewater Hunters*, spearfisherman Carlos Eyles said, "I've long since ceased taking full credit for the fish the ocean provides. The ocean is too vast, rich, and powerful an entity for me to assume that in any way I have conquered it. At best the effort is cooperative with nature supplying the sustenance and I the means to capture it. When the land was as bountiful as the ocean the hunting peoples understood the enormous and benevolent power of nature and became connected to that power through the animals they hunted."

There seems to be a universal human desire to transcend one's consciousness and reconnect with the universe or experience spirituality and soulfulness through immersion. Connection to and communication with the larger world beyond ourselves and "oneness" is what nearly all people are ultimately looking for. That is especially true during the legacy stage of life.

After spending two years at Walden, Thoreau decided it was time to move on. Even communing with nature and having a spiritual awakening could eventually lead to ending up in a rut, he concluded. "I left the woods for as good a reason as I went there. Perhaps it seemed to me that I had several more lives to live, and could not spare any more time for that one. It is remarkable how easily we fall into a particular route. I had not lived there a week before my feet wore a path from my door to the pond. And though it is five or six years since I trod it, it is still quite distinct. I fear others may have fallen into it. How deep the ruts of tradition and conformity!"

## What Is My Destiny?

World War II soldier Kurt Vonnegut was captured and only survived the bombing of Dresden because he was imprisoned in a slaughterhouse's meat locker. After the war he adopted his sister's four sons after she died of cancer and her husband was killed in a train accident in a span of just two days. Vonnegut became a novelist, and his writing is informed by the profound impact terrible events had on his life. In his most popular novel, *Slaughterhouse Five*, a soldier receives no awards for his heroism, but is put to death by firing squad for stealing a teapot. In his novels and in comments on current events, such as the assassination of Robert F. Kennedy, Vonnegut often used the phrase, "So it goes..."

This was his shorthand way of saying the universe is indifferent to what happens to us. There are no supernatural powers watching after us like guardians. We are all buffeted continuously by random forces, and regardless of whether good or bad things happen to us, life goes on. This general view of the way the world operates is consistent with this book. If passing through the five life stages—adventure, mission, family, tribe, and legacy—and fully experiencing them is to mean anything, we can't believe that a predetermined destiny external to us is forcing us down a specific path. We must believe we can make our own choices and act upon them.

The Bible and the Koran also counsel their adherents to look after themselves and not leave everything to God. Even Jesus struggled and was tempted in his early years and had to make difficult decisions at the end of his life. Any successes that are meaningful and any improvement in the condition of our lives must be generated from within ourselves and be implemented through our actions and choices.

No external forces are loading the dice for us to be successful, nor are any such forces actively trying to prevent us from achieving our goals. We have to create our own destinies through our choices during each of the five life stages. We'll need to overcome difficult events and embrace random good fortune. We have to nudge our destinies in the direction we wish by not allowing these factors to take us off our chosen course:

- *Suffering*. Most religions teach that life is suffering, and Buddhism proposes that we avoid suffering. Instead, choose to embrace suffering strategically along the mission path, as the greatest moments in our lives come immediately after immense suffering.
- *Consumption*. Western consumerism entices people to consume as much as they can, while communism wants everyone to consume equally. Instead, choose not to accumulate or consume more than is required by your mission, your family and your tribe.
- *Conflict*. Modern societies have laws, police forces, and armies to resolve conflicts and keep the peace. Instead, choose to see that conflict is a symptom of resource imbalances and ensure your personal and tribal missions don't add to imbalances.
- *Afterlife*. Most religions want their adherents to trade an unpleasant current life for a pleasant afterlife. Instead, choose to live life to the fullest now, but seek fulfillment rather than happiness. Provide for your family and your tribe, and live on through your legacy.
- *Ideology*. Institutions and philosophical movements like capitalism and communism want to indoctrinate people into their ideology. Choose instead to reject ideology and build your life around executing a mission and legacy that improves the world.

Some people want to know *What is my destiny?* as though it is one discrete thing. But in fact, it is five things. Our destinies are what we choose to create in the form of having great adventures, pursuing personally important missions, loving our families, leading our tribes, and leaving useful legacies to those who will remain after we are gone.

## Life Cycle of the "Self"

"David Bowie's Music Catalogue Sold to Warner Music for $250M," read a Reuters headline in 2022. Fans and non-fans alike were staggered by the number. With the passing of rock stars like David Bowie, George Harrison, and Freddie Mercury, an entire generation of iconic musicians is being forced to confront their mortality.

Older rock stars, like Bruce Springsteen, who was born in 1949 and began performing as a guitar hero in New Jersey when he was just a teenager, are being more thoughtful than ever in enhancing and preserving their legacies. They are releasing commemorative editions, creating comprehensive box sets, and putting a lot of care into their concert set lists. Springsteen is a prime example of how rock stars go through phases as their careers develop. In the 1970s Springsteen and his E Street Band were young New Jersey go-getters, crashing on couches and living hand-to-mouth. They eventually found commercial success with their spirited and biographical third album, *Born to Run*.

In the 1980s Springsteen experienced mass popularity with *Born in the USA*, featuring pop songs and dance tunes. Springsteen tried in the 1990s to move back to grittier songs, but his albums lacked the autobiographical themes beloved by his fans in his earlier work. Then in the 2000s, Springsteen went back to his origins with the more personal *Wrecking Ball*. He recaptured his fans and tied his boyhood idol, Elvis Presley, for the most number-one albums of all time by a solo artist.

Of these different career phases and personas, Springsteen has said: "Whoever you've been and wherever you've been, it never leaves you. I always picture it as a car. All your selves are in it. A new self can get in, but the old selves can't ever get out. The important thing is, who's got their hands on the wheel at any given moment?"

Unlike a rock star, a newborn baby doesn't have a "self" or realize it is a separate from its surroundings. As she grows into a toddler, she begins to comprehend herself as distinct from her environment, but continues to have no sense of self-awareness as adults define it. As she grows older, she doesn't wish to be perceived as a toddler, so she tries to influence others to view her as strong, smart, and independent. This is the beginning of the construction of a self in the outside world and in the child's mind.

In the world of infants and animals, there is no self. A tiger is an extension of its environment. A human baby or tiger cub sleeps, eats, and poops whenever and wherever it chooses, unconcerned with how another tiger or human perceives it. It acts in order to seek pleasure and protects its body. Adult humans seek pleasure and to protect their physical bodies too, but they also go to great lengths to project a favorable self-image to the external world of other people. They will work to protect their self if it is threatened by insult or loss of reputation. Hopefully during the adventure stage of life, you learned that you *are* your behavior and to focus your efforts on behavior (which is core) rather than on self (which is projection).

An elder comes to see that during a younger time in their life, the exertion of effort needed to project a self was to some extent unavoidable during the process of formulating and pursuing and achieving a mission. But now the mission has given way to legacy, and the self becomes of less value, and in some cases a hindrance, as an elder seeks to preserve their legacy.

Springsteen began an even more open and candid autobiographical phase in 2016. His memoir, *Born to Run*, was a bestseller. *Springsteen on Broadway* brought his music to his fans in a theater setting. And in *Western Stars* he performed his best-known songs with heartfelt introductions, explaining their origins. In 2022 he sold his music catalogue for $500 million. Even formerly rebellious unconventional rock stars can feel a deep urge to move beyond the self and work to carefully preserve their legacies.

**Casting Away the Self**

"Get on the ground!" the game warden yelled, aiming his gun at the burglar's nose and blinding him with his flashlight. After years of detective work the warden had finally apprehended the North Pond Hermit, who had been breaking into homes and camps in heavily wooded central Maine. As Michael Finkel wrote in a 2014 article for *GQ* magazine, this night was a typical robbery for the hermit, who had stuffed his backpack with marshmallows, potato chips, and bacon. Hardly grand theft.

But what came to light from this arrest shocked the world. The hermit had a name, Christopher Knight, and he had been living in the woods in a hidden encampment he built within a rock formation since he was 20, way back in 1986. For the past 27 years he had been living by himself and robbing nearby residents to obtain food and supplies. Tonight was the first time in almost three decades he had spoken with another human being.

When author Michael Finkel visited Knight in jail, he was eager to know what Knight had learned about himself and the human condition after so many years of living alone. Knight told him, "I did examine myself. Solitude did increase my perception. But here's the tricky thing: When I applied my increased perception to myself, I lost my identity. With no audience, no one to perform for, I was just there. There was no need to define myself; I became irrelevant. I didn't even have a name. I never felt lonely. To put it romantically: I was completely free."

This explanation from Knight about how he lived for 27 years devoid of an identity, a name, or a "self" is somehow haunting and disturbing to those of us who live within modern society with our selves bumping into and interacting with many other selves every day. It serves to demonstrate that the whole artifice of the self is so flimsy that given separation from other people for a period of time it can disappear.

While in the adventure stage of life you learned about the *existential fallacy*, which occurs when an actor crosses the line and loses themself in their onstage creation. A person and their self are similar to an actor and their role, and this insight is helpful in developing good manners with others through treating their "illusion of self" with care.

Now in the elder stage of life, with one's mission completed, a related concept is worth considering. *Aesthetic distance* refers to the gap between a person's conscious reality and the reality presented in a work of art. Or to say it another way, an actor is not the character they are playing in a play or movie, and a person is not their executed mission once they pass through and beyond the mission stage.

The "self" to an elder is like a part to an actor after a play is over. Its purpose has been served. The doctrine of most forms of religion and spirituality lead to a central premise that "everything is one," or *oneness*. At the deepest level within nearly all people is a desire to feel a connection to the totality of humankind, nature, and the universe. In this regard, to search through the self for a universal connection and for wisdom is a dead end. It is the core essence of a person, not the self that is attached to the whole world.

As Knight was about to be released from jail he said something else disturbing and haunting. He was speaking about his own apprehensiveness rather than trying to offer a critique of our society. But his words capture his rebuke of our selves in the aggregate:

"I don't know your world," Knight said. "Only my world, and memories of the world before I went into the woods. What is life today? What is proper? I have to figure out how to live. I miss the woods. Sitting here in jail, I don't like what I see in the society I'm about to enter. I don't think I'm going to fit in. It's too loud. Too colorful. The lack of aesthetics. The crudeness. The inanities. The trivia."

## I Hand You My Dream

From Normandy, which was originally a Viking base, "William the Bastard" led his fleet's invasion of England in 1066. William was a Norman nobleman, a burly and strong fighter with great stamina, and an excellent horseman. He instructed his army to pretend to flee, but then upon his signal they launched a counterattack. On English soil the Normans defeated Harold Godwinson's army in the Battle of Hastings. With Godwinson dead, William was crowned king on Christmas Day. He became the first Norman king of England, and thereafter he was known as William the Conqueror.

William spent the rest of his life consolidating his rule over all of England. Eventually Normans replaced the entire Anglo-Saxon aristocracy, but William retained most of England's institutions, including the church. When he died in 1087, his son William inherited England and became its new king. Every king or queen of England since William the Conqueror has been his direct descendant, making the British Monarchy a royal dynasty almost a thousand years old.

An inheritance to one's descendants is one type of legacy that nearly all people with children will leave. In most cases this legacy may be family heirlooms with sentimental value, some pieces of jewelry or collectible items, or a small amount of money. But leaving your career to your heir and expecting them to spend their life running it is a completely different proposition.

Philip of Macedon left his well-trained armies to his son Alexander, which Alexander used to conquer the world. Howard Hughes Sr. passed down his tool company and drilling patents to his son Howard Jr., which Howard Jr. used for cashflow for his movie and aviation endeavors, and became the wealthiest man in the world. Robert Turner left his son Ted his billboard company, which Ted grew into a global broadcasting conglomerate and used to make the world's first billion-dollar philanthropic pledge. And William the Conqueror bequeathed the English Monarchy to his son William, which William kept intact through his descendants, a succession still going strong nearly a millennium later.

Leaving your descendants the keys to the family business or some valuable material assets are noble gestures. But consider the following questions if you have a legacy goal of "handing your dream" to your heirs:

- *Are you choosing their life for them?* As Marv Marinovich learned with his son, you can't choose another person's immortality project for them. And as Doc Paskowitz learned, you may turn your children against you if you choose their lives for them. People who don't craft their own lifepath may suffer debilitating depression.

- *Are you sure they won't drop the baton?* Relay races can be lost if the baton is bobbled or dropped during the handoff. Trying to hand an operating platform to heirs who are too young or unsure of what they are getting into can be extremely risky. Will your descendants tarnish your good work and undo your legacy of accomplishments?

- *Are you buying their participation?* Are you using legacy gifts as a means of control from beyond the grave to compel your descendants to do what you want them to do? Are you trying to control your own kids and future generations rather than trusting them to make good decisions and do what they want?

If your legacy gifts contain an explicit or implicit "I hand you my dream" component, recognize that it can be either a blessing or burden to put on another person. In his youth, Howard Hughes was a scratch golfer and dreamed of becoming a professional. Ted Turner was on the Brown University sailing team, and sailing was his primary passion in life. We can never know what either would have done if left to make their own choices.

## Top-Five Bucket List

"Carter and I saw the world together, which is amazing when you think that only three months ago, we were complete strangers. I hope that it doesn't sound selfish of me, but the last months of his life were the best months of mine."

The expression *kick the bucket* means "to die," so a "bucket list" is a list of things a person wants to do or experience before the end of their life. In the 2007 movie *The Bucket List*, two terminally ill cancer patients, Carter and Edward, hatch a plan to break out of the hospital and spend their last days living life to the fullest. One is a mechanic and the other is a billionaire, so ostensibly they have little in common, other than a desire to accomplish a list of goals before they die and find out once and for all who they really are.

Thanks to Edward's wealth and his private jet, they are able to globe-trot and attack their bucket lists with zeal and in style. They go skydiving, race a Shelby Mustang, fly over the North Pole, travel to the Taj Mahal, go to Mount Everest, ride motorcycles on the Great Wall of China, go on safari in Africa, and visit the top of the Great Pyramid in Egypt.

If you search "top 10 bucket list" online, here is a list of people's top 10 items for their bucket lists ranked in order of most votes received:

Top Ten Bucket List

- See the northern lights
- Go on a cruise
- Swim with dolphins
- Go skydiving
- Visit the pyramids
- Get married

- Go scuba diving
- Buy a house
- Run a marathon
- Go ziplining

These items from both the *Bucket List* movie and the online list, (other than "get married" and "buy a house"), could be retitled, "have adventures." And that brings us back to the beginning. You have a bucket list too. But it doesn't have 10 items on it. Your list has five: have adventures, choose mission, start family, lead tribe, and leave legacy. And fortunately, you have been working on your bucket list continuously throughout your entire adult life rather than saving it until the end.

You can always go back to your bucket list, even in the legacy stage. Hopefully you pursued a series of fantastic adventures in your youth, but if there were some you missed due to finances or other commitments, consider doing what Edward and Carter did. If your mission still has some aspects that have not been completed, or if there are loose ends to tie up, you can attend to those too. It would be nice if you still maintained some connections to your old tribe, visiting with your former lieutenants and your people.

But more than likely, if you find yourself terminally ill as Edward and Carter did, it will be your family and your legacy that most command your attention. Hopefully you will be surrounded by family if you are weak and debilitated. And alternatively, if you are well enough to pursue adventures, maybe you'll be on safari or racing Mustangs with your spouse or children or both, ticking items off your bucket lists together. You will have already passed through and experienced the first four life stages, and will be endeavoring to the end to put the final touches on your legacy.

As Carter says in *The Bucket List*: "You know, the ancient Egyptians had a beautiful belief about death. When their souls got to the entrance to heaven, the guards asked two questions. Their answers determined whether they were able to enter or not. 'Have you found joy in your life?' and 'Has your life brought joy to others?'" If we pressed Carter, he would probably agree that these two questions could better be translated from Egyptian using the word *fulfillment* rather than *joy*.

**Finding Oneness**

There was a batter who stopped and made the sign of the cross on his chest prior to stepping into the batter's box. He swung and missed three times and sulked off. The pitcher pumped his fist to celebrate the strikeout before pointing up at the heavens and mouthing, "Thank you."

Was God, with long, flowing, silvery hair, lounging on a cloud above the stadium, watching that duel and orchestrating the outcome like a magician? Was the universe on the side of either player? Is there a mystical energy field that a pitcher or batter can make offerings to, or negotiate with, in exchange for a hit or a strikeout?

Is there a divine being or an external fate that guides everything? Or, is it that whomever is in charge—God, the universe, Mother Nature, karma, the Force, ancient aliens, the Matrix—is indifferent to the smaller day-to-day matters of our lives such as one at-bat? When we feel we're having an external mystical experience, is the experience actually internal to us?

A spearfisherman surrounded by fish, sharks, kelp, and crashing waves matches his movements to the current. A hiker surrounded by trees, wildlife, wind, and sunshine adjusts her steps to the slope of the mountain. A batter surrounded by the opposing team and the jeering of the hometown crowd matches his tempo to the pitcher. Sensitivity to the power of the fish/currents, or the wind/terrain or the pitcher/crowd allow us to go into a meditative state, lose ourselves and tap into *oneness* with the world.

There are many paths to tapping the unity of the world, or oneness:

- *The Christians call it spirit*. A force or principle believed to animate humans and often to endure after departing from the body of a person at death.
- *The Buddhists call it "dharma."* The idea of a law or principle governing the universe. For an individual to live out their dharma is to act in accordance with this law and is the path to enlightenment.
- *The Hindus call it "jana."* Spiritual knowledge or wisdom of the self that is inseparable from the Divine, rather than worldly knowledge that is obtained through learning or experience.
- *The Chinese call it "tao."* The absolute principle underlying the universe, combining the principles of yin and yang and signifying the way or code of behavior that is in harmony with the natural order.
- *The Greeks call it "logos."* A universal divine reason immanent in nature, yet transcending all oppositions and imperfections in the cosmos and humanity. An eternal and unchanging truth.
- *The Muslims call it "ruh."* An agent of divine action or communication issuing from command of God, which is considered the source of human life.

Among all people there is a deep thirst for belief systems that have oneness as their center spoke. This is because oneness can address our desire to maintain a connection to the world of the living that endures after death. Oneness helps us recognize we are each a part of a vast river of humanity. A river that birthed us and sustains us. A river that flowed millions of years ago, and to which we are contributing now through our missions and legacies. It becomes easier to release our physical bodies when we realize that even after we die we will remain part of this ever expanding and timeless river.

Immortality can be found by embracing oneness. Our belief systems—religion, mythology, spirituality, and philosophy—each tell us a similar story: life ends with death, fear makes us want to overcome death, we can defeat death by joining something so large it will endure after we die.

## Grant Them Immortality

Musashi knew Kojiro would defeat and kill him in the sword duel that was to take place on Ganryujima island. And he was at peace with that. Kojiro, with his oversized samurai sword (called "the washing pole") and his overhead strike technique was undefeated and considered to be unbeatable.

As he meditated long into the night, a strategy occurred to Musashi. The duel was set to begin at 8 a.m., the "dragon hour," but Musashi intentionally arrived by boat two hours late. As he had expected, Kojiro was onshore, enraged by this insult. Musashi leaped from the boat. Instead of his usual two steel dueling swords, he wielded a wooden oar he had carved into a sword even longer than Kojiro's during the passage. Each samurai swung at the other simultaneously. Musashi had chosen the perfect hour, and the sun was behind his back as he had planned. Kojiro was blinded by it. The tip of his blade sliced Musashi's headband in half and it fell to the ground. Musashi's blow struck Kojiro's head squarely and killed him.

Ganruyjima is now considered the most famous samurai duel of all time. It occurred in 1612 when Musashi was about 30. With his trademark humility, Musashi said later: "When I reached thirty, I looked back on my past. The previous victories were not due to my having mastered strategy. Perhaps it was natural ability, or the order of heaven, or that the other school's strategy was inferior. After that I studied morning and evening searching for the principle and came to realize the way of strategy when I was fifty."

Miyamoto Musashi was the greatest samurai swordsman of all time, and founded the Niten Ichi-Ryu school of swordsmanship. Using his double-sword technique, he won 61 duels and was never defeated. Later in life, in his fifties and dying from cancer, Musashi went to Reigando Cave to meditate and write *A Book of Five Rings*.

The book is his legacy, containing everything he had learned of sword dueling, the way of strategy, and how to approach life. After two years Musashi had completed the manuscript, and he died in the cave a few months later, in 1645. His book is revered to this day by Japanese martial artists and businesspeople as a national treasure.

To leave a legacy is to plant a tree. Trees outlive people. And after the person who planted the tree is long dead, any number of people far out into the future can enjoy the shade and fruit of that tree. For the Japanese people, Musashi's tree is still alive and well.

Musashi achieved his mission of becoming the greatest living swordsman. For him and his peers, to be a samurai swordsman was not a job or a career, it was a calling and a lifestyle. There is no retiring from a lifestyle. On the contrary, the life retired him. When he realized his skill had become so great that he had achieved his mission and was invincible, he began fighting with wooden swords only. And he planted a tree by founding his swordsmanship school. And he planted another tree by writing *The Book of Five Rings*. And then, with his legacy complete, he died.

When we think of legacy, we tend to think of our own legacy and our present time rather than what our legacy will mean to future generations. In order to think across generations, the "legacy as tree" metaphor is useful. It allows us to visualize how our legacies can benefit and inspire people we will never meet. People born long after we have passed on can enjoy the shade of the trees we have planted.

Musashi left his writing. Beethoven left his music. Picasso left his art. As you think about your legacy, take some time. Sit in the cool shade of a tall tree that is a century old, or perhaps even older. Read Musashi's teachings. Listen to Beethoven's melodies. Look at Picasso's compositions. Breathe and reflect. Allow the presence of these greats and their legacies to wash over you. Grant them the immortality they so rightfully deserve.

## An Unknown Destination

"The Shaman...he was a man who would intoxicate himself...he would put himself into a trance... Then he would go on a mental travel and... describe his journey to the rest of the tribe." Said Jim Morrison—lead singer of the Doors—to *New York Magazine* journalist Richard Goldstein in 1968. He was attempting to explain the haunting, dark, hypnotic, and apocalyptical lyrics of "The End". Was he suggesting that he had traveled like a shaman to the afterlife and brought a song about it back to the living?

"The End" is an epic rock ballad by the 1960s American band the Doors. It evolved through months of jam-style performances at the Whisky a Go Go nightclub in Los Angeles in 1966 into a much longer song. A nearly 12-minute version was released in 1967. It was famously used in the iconic opening scene of Francis Ford Coppola's 1979 film *Apocalypse Now*, and also again at the end of the film. The central theme of "The End" seems to be people's lives coming to an end, and moving on to whatever comes after.

In a 1969 interview with *Rolling Stone*, Doors lead singer Jim Morrison said the song means something different every time he listened to it. "I think it's sufficiently complex and universal in its imagery that it could be almost anything you want it to be." In other words, the song is intentionally vague, and an invitation to each listener to consider the themes of anything, and everything, including life, ultimately coming to an end.

Listen to the first few minutes of "The End" as you read the rest of this chapter. It is sweeping and cinematic as though the listener is traveling down a long, slowly moving river toward an unknown destination. As you listen, reflect upon the following themes:

- Let your mind wander through your past. Remember all the best and brightest parts in vivid detail. Release any bad memories.

- Your life was as it was supposed to be. It was at times exhilarating and magical, and at other times it was tragic and exasperating.

- You were never motivated by winning or money in and of themselves. The feeling of improvement brought you fulfillment.

- You followed your own unique path and used your special talents to be the best at what you cared most about.

- You now no longer need to protect your "self." Release all your anxieties and cares so that you can be free.

- You lived in the only meaningful way one can, by riding the river through all the life stages to find out what it was all about.

- You did the best you could. Be proud of what you accomplished and the people you helped. Now you are free to ride off into the sunset.

As you learned during the mission stage of life, all works of art, including our lives, are an expression of our ideas meant to produce something interesting, beautiful, and valuable to others. As you also learned during the mission stage, all projects including our lives have three phases: planning, execution, and closing. By the time any project, whether small and trivial or gigantic and vitally important, is in the closing stage, the project manager can't wait for it to be finished and done. At the end of any project or work of art, including our lives, we want to be able to truthfully say, "That was a blast, I couldn't have enjoyed it more, and I wouldn't change a thing—but I'm ready for it to come to an end."

When you complete your task of experiencing all five of the life stages, hopefully the end of the river will have brought you to exactly where you are supposed to be. And as Jim Morrison sings in "The End," you will find that the world truly is "limitless and free…"

## Who Will Miss Me?

"Why are you dying, Mama?" Forrest asked Mama Gump, who was resting in bed peacefully. She smiled and replied: "It's my time. It's just my time. Now don't you be afraid, sweetheart. Death is just a part of life. It's something we're all destined to do. I will miss you, Forrest."

Deathbed scenes in movies and books rarely work. They are prone to being melodramatic and riddled with clichés. Mama Gump's death scene in *Forrest Gump* is one of the best, because she and Forrest both accept what is going to happen. They are at peace with it, and don't try to fight it.

In 2000, *Publishers Weekly* listed *Charlotte's Web* as the best-selling children's paperback of all time. One likely reason it was such a loved book is that it has one of the saddest yet most deftly written "losing a loved one" scenes in all of literature. In this classic, which is for both children and adults, Charlotte the spider uses her webs and her writing skills to save the life of her friend, Wilbur the pig.

Right up to the very end of her life, she is focused on saving Wilbur's life, even though she herself has reached the end of her lifespan. Weakened, she dies, but Wilbur watches over her egg sac until her eggs hatch. Throughout the novel, Wilbur is terrified of death, but Charlotte knows that life is a cycle. She understands that she will live on through her children, and author E. B. White focuses his storytelling on the effect Charlotte's death has on others rather than how she feels about it.

If you were gone, who would miss you? How would your absence affect other people? Well before you get to that point, consider taking the following actions:

- *Remember who you really are.* Go back through your photos, letters, papers, and journals from when you were young all the way up to the present. Use these old images and papers and correspondence to remind you of who you really are and more importantly, who was truly important in your life.

- *Relationships, not achievements.* When you completed the mission stage of life, your achievements were made permanent. Now as an elder in the legacy stage of life, it is your relationships that matter. Reconnect with family, friends, and people from your tribe, and thank them. Forgive people who wronged you.

- *Don't leave a legacy of clutter.* You've had an entire lifetime of amazing experiences and accomplishments. Don't let what you've learned be lost. Write it down or share it with loved ones in person. Don't leave behind boxes of files and collections of stuff for the people you love, or loose ends that are a burden for them.

- *Work backwards from RIP.* If you were to leave this world today, what would prevent you from resting in peace? Whose tools have you forgotten to return? To what school or organization do you need to provide a gift? Who from long ago do you need to track down and thank? Whose forgiveness do you need to seek?

Charlotte's deathbed scene with Wilbur is as good as there's ever been in any movie or book. "Why did you do all this for me?" Wilbur asked Charlotte, "I don't deserve it. I've never done anything for you."

"You have been my friend," replied Charlotte. "That in itself is a tremendous thing. I wove my webs for you because I liked you. After all, what's a life anyway? We're born, we live a little while, we die. A spider's life can't help being something of a mess, with all this trapping and eating flies."

Enjoy the ride. Participate wholeheartedly and learn all you can. Fulfill your obligations. Leave something valuable behind. And exit stage left before you overstay your welcome.

## Rejoining the Source

> *"Every man's life ends the same way. It is only the details of how he lived and how he died that distinguish one man from another."*
> —Ernest Hemingway

Ernest Hemingway kept a piece of shrapnel as a good-luck charm. It was from a mortar shell that wounded him during World War I. If he had been more seriously injured by that shell, the world would have been denied one of its greatest writers. Because he had faced his own mortality so early in his life, death is a recurring theme in his writing. The characters in his novels—soldiers, fishermen, boxers, hunters—live an authentic life by demonstrating grace under pressure and by meeting death with courage and dignity.

For those of us who are fortunate enough to progress as elders well into the legacy stage, our vitality will eventually begin to diminish. We will find ourselves moving a little more slowly and our bodies aching a bit more with each passing year.

We are not yet on death's doorstep, but we can't help notice that our circle of friends continues to grow smaller. We seem to be attending more funerals than weddings. We might live another ten years, but we might also be felled at some point by a heart attack or a severe case of pneumonia. After so many years as "indestructible" adventurers and chieftains, death has finally become real to us.

"Try to learn to breathe deeply, really to taste food when you eat, and when you sleep, really to sleep," said Hemingway. "Try as much as possible to be wholly alive with all your might, and when you laugh, laugh like hell. And when you get angry, get good and angry. Try to be alive. You will be dead soon enough."

When death does finally catch up to us—perhaps at the end of a protracted battle with a chronic illness—we must view it as one last life stage. And though we are in a weakened state, we must treat death as we did the previous stages. We must bravely *perform* death, both for ourselves and for those family and friends who have assembled around us to witness our departure. With our missions behind us, we must surrender our legacies to the universe. This is our offering. A connecting link between ourselves and the world that will continue on after we are gone.

Surrounded by those we love most we can transfer to them the responsibility for nurturing and protecting the family and tribe. Because of the way we taught them and have guided them, they will be okay now without us. Both our ancestors and future generations are proud of us. If we have lived well, we have earned the right to fully let go now and continue on into the void and onwards to whatever comes next.

Take pride in saying, "I'm thankful that I did attain some worldly successes, that I did my best to live in harmony with other people and with nature, that I continuously sought enlightenment, and that I provided resources to the less fortunate. And all of that was made possible because I spent my years continuously and wholeheartedly pursuing fulfillment through adventures, mission, family, tribe, and legacy. Which, I believe, was the best way for me to have chosen to live my life."

Now in the final epic moments of our lives we can experience the ultimate fulfillment, the joy of rejoining the source and "going home." After the fullness of our lives, only death is left for us to experience. And having lived well—testing ourselves through adventures, bending the world to our will through our missions, nurturing a family, and stewarding a tribe—we can now embrace death as completely as we embraced life.

Through the good works of our legacies, we will continue on. Eternally.

## GLOSSARY OF LIFEPATH TERMS

**Adventure:** Taking a calculated risk in exchange for fun and self-knowledge that will be useful in carrying out the later four life stages.

**Art:** An expression of an artist's imaginative and conceptual ideas intended to be appreciated for their beauty and emotional power. Missions are both works of art and projects.

**Character:** A personal commitment to do what is right at all times, even if to do so comes at great personal cost. A person of good character makes choices and takes action based on internalized constant principles.

**Chieftain:** In modern times a chieftain forms a tribe in order to obtain assistance from people they trust in executing their mission on a larger scale than they could on their own. The chieftain is responsible for directing and overseeing the activities of tribe members, inspiring the tribe, and providing members an opportunity to earn income, learn skills, and have more autonomy than they would if they worked for an institution.

**Confrontation:** Using deception and manipulation—bluffing and posturing to affect an adversary's behavior in the search for an area of weakness—and acting with force if necessary (as opposed to negotiation, which is based on truth).

**Depression:** Experiencing a condition of sadness, of the absence of motivation, low energy, and difficulty making decisions. Lack of fulfillment can lead to depression. And depression can interfere with our ability to live a good life by performing the five life stages well.

**Destiny:** Belief that God or the universe or some other external force has a plan for everything and that a person's life is predetermined. (As opposed to belief in free will and self-determination.)

**Free Will:** Belief that a person's life is the result of decisions made of their own choices plus the influence of external random events and arbitrary circumstances. (As opposed to belief in fate or destiny.)

**Fulfillment:** The absence of depression. The culmination of extreme exertion toward a personally meaningful project of some form that advances the objectives of one or more of the five life stages. (Distinct from happiness or joy, which usually involve consumption.)

**Greatness:** Choosing to live by an internal code of character and pursue excellence in one's deeds rather than seeking personal perfection.

**Immortality Project:** Term coined by anthropologist Ernest Becker. The only way for a person to avoid debilitating neurosis from knowing death awaits us is to create a personalized *immortality project* that will live on after we die. This allows us to "cheat death." (Most missions are immortality projects.)

**Institution:** A group that at one point was a tribe, but has now grown to a size such that not all the members are able to know one another. Tribes tend to grow to 100 or so members before either breaking into several tribes, growing into an institution, or being acquired or absorbed by an institution.

**Laloki:** As used in these pages, to be "in Laloki" is to be superficially 'in paradise,' but actually to be in a depressed limbo state. E.g., Errol Flynn at his New Guinea plantation, or Humphrey Bogart at his Casablanca nightclub.

**Legacy:** A person's mission transitions into and becomes replaced by their legacy. What all forms of legacy have in common is that they serve as an enduring contribution that a person expects will live on after their death. In this way, all forms of legacy are an attempt at immortality through maintaining a connection to the living.

**Life Stages:** Roughly speaking there are five life stages, which overlap at times and so are not fully sequential: adventure, mission, tribe, family, legacy.

**Lifepath:** Traversing the five life stages, performing each to the best of our abilities, and thereby experiencing continuous personal fulfillment.

**Magic:** Wielding superpowers or supernatural knowledge via secret rituals to gain advantage over the natural world and other humans.

**Mentor:** A caring and experienced person who assists a protégé eight to 25 years their junior with making progress in their chosen field.

**Mission:** A personal project and calling that a person makes their top priority over a sustained period of their life. The choice of mission is informed by adventures during earlier stages of life. (Most missions are immortality projects.)

**Mission Track:** Continuous progress along the mission track leads to fulfillment and is the tightrope between depression and being "wrecked by success."

**Negotiation:** Using the truth to create a position of strength by presenting the most favorable facts in the best possible light in order to persuade an adversary and agree to terms (as opposed to confrontation, which is often based on deception).

**Oneness:** There seems to be a universal human desire to transcend one's consciousness and experience connection with the larger world outside ourselves. Different religions and philosophies use a variety of words to label and describe oneness.

**Philosophy:** Contemplation, analysis, and intellection aimed at answering eternal questions such as *How can I live a good life?*

**Project:** A temporary mobilization of resources that produces a deliverable. Missions are both projects and works of art.

**Professional:** A professional has made a commitment to perform at the top level of skill and performance at their chosen activity and be paid for doing so. (An amateur does the best they can, but is a part-timer.)

**Purposeful Addiction:** Choosing to go deep into a personally important activity for a sustained period of time in order to make a transcendent breakthrough. Humankind makes quantum leaps via purposeful addictions: Buddha (enlightenment), the Wright brothers (inventing flight), Isaac Newton (developing laws of motion).

**Religion:** Organized spirituality with clergy, special texts, and rituals teaching how to be a good person and have a pleasant afterlife.

**Scarce Resources:** The resources humans need to live—land, food, fuel—are valuable because they are limited. Competition for these scarce resources drives human life and human history. Success is measured by besting competitors and enjoyed by sharing surplus resources with loved ones.

**Soulfulness:** A spiritual awakening. Seeing deeply and experiencing appreciation for what we may call the universe, nature, destiny, karma, or God.

Arises when we spend long blocks of time totally immersed by ourselves in doing something, alone with our thoughts without interruption.

**Science:** Endeavoring to explain the natural world by formulating rules and laws that apply universally.

**Tribe:** A group of between 30 and 100 people united by a common mission, overseen by a chieftain. A tribe is large enough that each member can specialize at specific tasks. A tribe is small enough that all the members are able to know and hold each other accountable for their actions. Tribes are larger than families and smaller than institutions.

**Wrecked by Success:** Term coined by psychologist Sigmund Freud. He explained it as a paradox whereby people become neurotic as a result of success. A person can perform effectively at the highest level as long as their objective is in front of them. But as soon as they actually complete their goal, they are unable to handle the white-hot glow of success that ensues.

# NOTES

## Chapter 1: Have Adventures

3 Goodall, Jane, *In the Shadow of Man*, Mariner Books, New York, 1971, pp. 21, 54.

5 Isaacson, Walter, *Steve Jobs*, Simon & Schuster, New York, 2011, pp. 45-49.

5 Editors, "Life-Changer for Steve Jobs," *The Economic Times*, Oct 7, 2011.

6 Stewart, Martha, *The Martha Rules*, MSLO Inc., USA, 2005, p. 4.

7 Lloyd, Carli, *When Nobody Was Watching*, Mariner, New York, 2017, p. 39.

8 Lloyd, Carli, *When Nobody Was Watching*, Mariner, New York, 2017, p. 50.

9 Flynn, Errol, *My Wicked, Wicked Ways*, Cooper Square Press, NY, 2003, pp. 66,78, 98-102.

10 Flynn, Errol, *My Wicked, Wicked Ways*, Cooper Square Press, NY, 2003, p. 106.

11 Carlisle, Belinda, *Lips Unsealed*, Three Rivers Press, New York, 2010, p. 47.

11 Doe, John, *Under the Big Black Sun*, Random House, New York, 2016, p. 16.

12 Ivie, Devon, "Go-Go's Could've Been Bigger," *Vulture*, October 29, 2021.

12 Carlisle, Belinda, *Lips Unsealed*, Three Rivers Press, New York, 2010, pp. 45, 49-51.

13 Yeager, Chuck, *YEAGER*, Bantam Books, New York, 1985, p. 84, 108.

14 Yeager, Chuck, *YEAGER*, Bantam Books, New York, 1985. p. 200.

15 Smith, Sean, *J.K. Rowling*, Made in the USA, Las Vegas, 2001, pp. 71-72.

16 Parker, James, "The Story of Jack and Neal," *The Atlantic*, April, 2022.

17 Hilton, Conrad, *Be My Guest*, Prentice-Hall, New Jersey, 1957, p. 107-109.

18 Hilton, Conrad, *Be My Guest*, Prentice-Hall, New Jersey, 1957, p. 110-111.

19 Stewart, Martha, *The Martha Rules*, MSLO Inc., USA, 2005, p. 13.

19 Christopher, Matt, *Michael Jordan*, Little Brown, New York, 1996, p. 71.

19 Jackson, Phil, *Eleven Rings*, Penguin Books, New York, 2013, pp. 81, 94, 99.

19 Frost, Ilana, "Martha Stewart and Snoop Dogg's Friendship Timeline," *People*, May 15, 2023.

21 Alexander, Caroline, *The Endurance*, Alfred A. Knopf, New York, 2006, pp. 3, 99, 120.

23 Patrick, Danica, *Danica – Crossing the Line*, Fireside, New York, 2006, pp. 71, 74.

24 Patrick, Danica, *Danica – Crossing the Line*, Fireside, New York, 2006, pp. 75, 87.

25 *The Wizard of Oz*, Warner Brothers, 1939.

27 Morgan, Chris, "Nadia Comaneci's Perfect 10," *Buzz*, July, 2021.

29 Furdyk, Brent, "Stars Who Lost Their Tempers," *Nikki Swift*, December, 2020.

31 Markham, Beryl, *West With the Night*, North Point Press, New York, 2013, p. 217.

32 Markham, Beryl, *West With the Night*, North Point Press, New York, 2013, pp. 217-218.

33 Musashi, Miyamoto, *A Book of Five Rings*, Overlook Press, New York, 1994, pp. 10, 15.

33 Williams, Ted, *The Science of Hitting*, Simon & Schuster, New York, 1986, p. 97.

34 Musashi, Miyamoto, *A Book of Five Rings*, Overlook Press, New York, 1994, pp. 53-54.

34 Williams, Ted, *The Science of Hitting*, Simon & Schuster, New York, 1986, pp. 22, 82.

35 Eyles, Carlos, *Last of the Blue Water Hunters*, Watersport Publishing, 1985, pp. 66, 87.

36 Eyles, Carlos, *Last of the Blue Water Hunters*, Watersport Publishing, 1985, p. 116.

38 Heller, Anne, *Ayn Rand and the World She Made*, Anchor Books, 2009, p. 161.

39 *Seinfeld*, NBC, 1990-1999.

39 Lewis, Michael, *Liar's Poker*, W.W. Norton & Company, New York, 1989, pp. 27, 51, 301.

40 *Wall Street*, 20th Century Fox, 1987.

## Chapter 2: Choose Mission

41 Smith, Sean, *J.K. Rowling*, Made in the USA, Las Vegas, 2001, pp. 81, 83, 111, 122.

42 Donald, David, *Lincoln*, Simon & Schuster, New York, 1995, pp. 362-364.

43 Forden, Sara, *House of Gucci*, Harper Collins, New York, 2021, p. 241.

45 Eyles, Carlos, *Last of the Blue Water Hunters*, Watersport Publishing, 1985, pp. 23-24.

46 Patrick, Danica, *Danica – Crossing the Line*, Fireside, New York, 2006, pp. 5, 8.

46 Hilton, Conrad, *Be My Guest*, Prentice-Hall, New Jersey, 1957, pp. 102-103.

47 Deresiewicz, William, *Excellent Sheep*, Free Press, New York, 2014, p. 1.

48 Deresiewicz, William, *Excellent Sheep*, Free Press, New York, 2014, p. 90.

49 Flynn, Errol, *My Wicked, Wicked Ways*, Cooper Square Press, New York, 2003.

50 Christopher, Matt, *Michael Jordan*, Little Brown, New York, 1996.

50 Flynn, Errol, *My Wicked, Wicked Ways*, Cooper Square Press, NY, 2003, pp. 102-105.

51 Molho, Renata, *Being Armani*, Baldini Castoldi Dalai, Milan, 2007, pp. 17-19, 22, 39-41.

52 Becker, Ernest, *The Denial of Death*, Free Press, New York, 1973, pp. 27, 57.

52 Molho, Renata, *Being Armani*, Baldini Castoldi Dalai, Milan, 2007, p. 157.

53 Lloyd, Carli, *When Nobody Was Watching*, Mariner, New York, 2017, pp. 2, 44, 50.

54 Williams, Ted, *The Science of Hitting*, Simon & Schuster, New York, 1986, p. 15.

55 Unger, Miles, *Michelangelo*, Simon & Schuster, New York, 2014, pp. 79-83.

56 Unger, Miles, *Michelangelo*, Simon & Schuster, New York, 2014, p. 91.

56 Keane, Thomas, *Project Management*, Made in USA, San Bernardino, 2018, pp. 3-4.

57 Unger, Miles, *Michelangelo*, Simon & Schuster, New York, 2014, pp. 94-95.

58 Rubin, Rick, *The Creative Act*, Penguin Press, New York, 2023, p. 144.

58 Unger, Miles, *Michelangelo*, Simon & Schuster, New York, 2014, pp. 105-107.

59 Stewart, Martha, *The Martha Rules*, MSLO Inc., USA, 2005, p. 7.

59 Manning, Mathew, *DC Comics Encyclopedia*, DK Publishing, New York, 2021, pp. 230, 298.

60 Foote, Brett, "Porsche 365 Rose From Ashes of Austrian Sawmill," *Rennlist*, Dec 10, 2019.
60 Molho, Renata, *Being Armani*, Baldini Castoldi Dalai, Milan, 2007, p. 65.
60 Stewart, Martha, *The Martha Rules*, MSLO Inc., USA, 2005, pp. 60-61.
61 Nakamura, Hajime, *Gotama Buddha*, Kosei Publishing, Tokyo, 2000, pp. 151-154.
62 Nakken, Craig, *The Addictive Personality*, Hazelden, Minnesota, 1986, pp. 20-21.
63 Kielty, Martin, "Van Halen's Last Roth Era Hit," *Ultimate Classic Rock*, June 19, 2019.
63 Hart, Michael, *The 100*, Carol Publishing, New York, 1994, pp. 99-100.
64 Hart, Michael, *The 100*, Carol Publishing, New York, 1994, pp. 66-68.
56 Rand, Ayn, *The Fountainhead*, Signet, New York, 1993, p. 201.
65 Isaacson, Walter, *Elon Musk*, Simon & Schuster, New York, 2023, p. 6.
66 Rand, Ayn, *The Fountainhead*, Signet, New York, 1993, p. 202.
67 Von Clausewitz, Carl, *On War*, Penguin Books, London, 1968, p. 241.
68 O'Malley, Zack, *Empire State of Mind*, Penguin, New York, 2021, p. 63.
69 Walsh, Bill, *The Score Takes Care of Itself*, Portfolio, New York, 2009, pp. 17, 160.
69 Dunnavant, Keith, *Montana*, Thomas Dunn Books, New York, 2009, pp. 90, 93.
70 Newman, Paul, *Paul Newman a Memoir*, Vintage Books, New York, 2023, p. 228.
71 Ivie, Devon," Angus Young on AC/DC," *Vulture,* December 11, 2020.
71 Masino, Susan, *AC/DC FAQ*, Backbeat Books, Milwaukee, WI, 2015, pp. 182-184.
72 Masino, Susan, *AC/DC FAQ*, Backbeat Books, Milwaukee, WI, 2015, pp. 270-274.
73 Fleming, Ian, *Moonraker*, Penguin Books, USA, 2003, p. 9.
75 Fox, Robin, *Alexander the Great*, Penguin Books, New York, 2004, pp. 59-62.
75 Hart, Michael, *The 100*, Carol Publishing, New York, 1994, pp. 174-178.
76 Carlson, Erin, *Queen Meryl*, Hachette Books, New York, 2019, p. 267.
77 Goldsworthy, Adrian, *Caesar*, Yale University Press, USA, 2006, pp. 100, 495, 502.
78 Beard, Mary, *SPQR: A History of Ancient Rome*, Liveright, New York, 2015, pp. 291-295.
78 Becker, Ernest, *The Denial of Death*, Free Press, New York, 1973, p. 49.
79 Madden, Steve, *The Cobbler*, Reading List Editorial, Canada, 2020, pp. 60, 81.
80 Au-Yeng, Angel, "Tony Hsieh's American Tragedy," *Forbes*, December, 2020.
80 Madden, Steve, *The Cobbler*, Reading List Editorial, Canada, 2020, p. 244.

## Chapter 3: Start Family

81 *Casablanca*, Warner Brothers, 1942.
82 *Casablanca*, Warner Brothers, 1942.
83 Forden, Sara, *House of Gucci*, Harper Collins, New York, 2021, pp. 58, 418.
84 Murakami, Haruki, *Novelist as Vocation*, Vintage, New York, 2022, pp. 25, 99-100.

85 Editors, *The Gazette*, "Transcript: Kurt Warner's Hall of Fame Speech," August 6, 2017.

86 Warner, Kurt, *All Things Possible*, Harper One, New York, 2009, p. 183.

87 *Mad Men*, AMC Original Productions, 2007-2015.

88 O'Malley, Zack, *Empire State of Mind*, Penguin, New York, 2021, p. 144.

89 *Meet the Parents*, Universal Pictures, 2000.

90 Theroux, Paul, *Hotel Honolulu*, Mariner Books, New York, 2002, p. 296.

91 *Lost in Translation*, Focus Features, 2003.

92 Fogerty, John, *Fortunate Son*, Hatchette Books, New York, 2016, p. 221.

92 *Lost in Translation*, Focus Features, 2003.

93 Christopher, Matt, *Tom Brady*, Little Brown, New York, 2018, p. 11.

93 Agassi, Andre, *Open: An Autobiography*, Vintage, 2009, pp. 1, 28, 70.

95 Based on a true story, with names and some details changed.

97 University Press (Editors), *Oprah Winfrey*, University Press, Las Vegas, 2021, pp. 4-5.

97 Kiyosaki, Robert, *Rich Dad Poor Dad*, Plata Publishing, AZ, 2017, pp. 9-10.

98 *The Karate Kid*, Columbia Pictures, 1984.

99 Laird, Sam, "The Tragic Rise and Fall of Marinovich," *Mashable*, Oct 15, 2016.

101 Gurdjieff, G., *Meetings with Remarkable Men*, Martino Publishing, CT, 2010, pp. 266-269.

105 Lynn, Kenneth, *Hemingway*, Simon and Schuster, New York, 1987, pp. 117-118.

106 Deresiewicz, William, *Excellent Sheep*, Free Press, New York, 2014, p. 42.

106 Phillips, Larry, *Ernest Hemingway on Writing*, Scribner, New York, 1984, p. 11.

107 *The Godfather*, Paramount, 1972.

108 Puzo, Mario, *The Godfather*, Berkley, New York, 2019, p. ix.

109 *Surfwise*, Magnolia Pictures, 2008.

110 Paskowitz, Izzy, *Scratching the Horizon*, St. Martin's Press, New York, 2012, pp. 33-52.

110 Zemler, Emily, "Morgan Freeman: What I've Learned," *Esquire*, March 3, 2016.

111 *Blow*, New Line Cinema, 2001.

112 Wooden, John, *Wooden on Leadership*, McGraw Hill, New York, 2005, pp. 36-37.

113 *The Big Chill*, Columbia Pictures, 1983.

115 Dumas, Alexandre, *The Three Musketeers*, Fp Classics, New York, 2023, p. 7.

116 *Forrest Gump*, Paramount Pictures, 1995.

117 *Taken*, 20th Century Fox, 2009.

118 Marche, Stephen, "A Very Particular Set of Skills," *Esquire*, January 8, 2015.

118 *Taken*, 20th Century Fox, 2009.

## Chapter 4: Lead Tribe

121 Foerster, Brien, *Easter Island The Secret Knowledge*, Made in the USA, 2021, pp. 3-4.

122 Thomas, Hugh, *Conquest: The Fall of Old Mexico*, Simon and Schuster, 1995, pp. 9-14.

123 Ngoy, Ted, *The Donut King*, Published by Ted Ngoy, CA, 2018, pp. 52-62.

125 Garelick, Rhonda, *Mademoiselle*, Random House, New York, 2015, pp. 126-128.

127 *The Adventures of Robin Hood*, Warner Brothers, 1939.

129 Forden, Sara, *House of Gucci*, Harper Collins, New York, 2021, pp. 29-31.

129 *Studio 54*, Netflix, 2018.

130 *Winchell's Donuts – The Rise and Fall*, Takeoutery, 2023.

131 Knight, Phil, *Shoe Dog*, Simon and Schuster, New York, 2016, pp. 281-285.

135 *The Life Aquatic With Steve Zissou*, Touchstone/Disney, 2004

136 Verducci, Tom, *The Cubs Way*, Crown Archetype, New York, 2017, P. 192.

137 *Apocalypse Now*, United Artists, 1979.

138 *Hearts of Darkness: A Filmmaker's Apocalypse*, Triton Pictures, 1991.

139 Kaufman, JB, The Fairest of them All, WDFF Press, USA, 2012, pp. 9, 31-33, 250.

139 Gabler, Neal, *Walt Disney*, Alfred Knopf, New York, 2006, pp. 207, 276-279.

139 Alba, Jessica, *The Honest Life*, Rodale Books, New York, 2013, pp. xiii-xix.

139 Phillips, Larry, *Ernest Hemingway on Writing*, Scribner, New York, 1984, p. 75.

141 *Bull Durham*, Metro Goldwyn Mayer, 1988.

142 *Bull Durham*, Metro Goldwyn Mayer, 1988.

143 *The Blues Brothers*, Universal Studios, 1980.

143 Matsushita, Konosuke, *People Before Products*, PHP Institute, Japan, 1992.

144 Matsushita, Konosuke, *People Before Products*, PHP Institute, Japan, 1992.

144 *The Blues Brothers*, Universal Studios, 1980.

145 *Casino*, Universal Studios, 1995.

146 Yeager, Chuck, *YEAGER*, Bantam Books, New York, 1985, pp. 369-370.

147 Finke, Nikki, "Oprah Winfrey Talks OWN Network," *Deadline*, Aug 16, 2013.

147 Beard, Mary, *SPQR: A History of Ancient Rome*, Liveright, New York, 2015, pp. 163, 255, 527.

148 Finke, Nikki, "Oprah Winfrey Talks OWN Network," *Deadline*, Aug 16, 2013.

149 Bergreen, Laurence, *Over the Edge of the World*, Harper Collins, 2003, pp. 281, 340, 391.

150 Hart, Michael, *The 100*, Carol Publishing, New York, 1994, pp. 79-80.

150 Swindoll, Charles, *Great Lives: Moses*, Thomas Nelson, New York, 2009.

151 Fortune Editors, "When Steve Met Bill," *Fortune*, October 23, 2011.

152 Isaacson, Walter, *Steve Jobs*, Simon & Schuster, New York, 2011, pp. 353-354.

153 Forden, Sara, *House of Gucci*, Harper Collins, New York, 2021, pp. 440-441, 450-458.
155 Stewart, Martha, *The Martha Rules*, MSLO Inc., USA, 2005, pp. 172-175.
155 Crichton, Michael, *Jurassic Park*, Ballantine Books, USA, 2015, pp. 110-111.
156 Welch, David, *Decisions, Decisions*, Prometheus Books, New York, 2002, pp. 32-44.
156 Hilton, Conrad, *Be My Guest*, Prentice-Hall, New Jersey, 1957, p. 63.
157 *10,000 BC*, Warner Brothers, 2008.
157 Hart, Michael, *The 100*, Carol Publishing, New York, 1994, pp. 514-515.
157 Jones, Brian, *George Lucas*, Little Brown & Company, New York, 2016, pp. 136, 197, 464.
159 Wooden, John, *Wooden on Leadership*, McGraw Hill, New York, 2005, pp. 73-75.

## Chapter 5: Leave Legacy

161 *24/7: Kelly Slater*, HBO Films, 2019.
163 Brown, Peter, *Howard Hughes*, First Da Capo Press, 2004, pp. 259, 373, 376.
165 University Press (Editors), *Oprah Winfrey*, University Press, Las Vegas, 2021, p. 52.
165 Napoli, Lisa, *Up All Night*, Abrams Press, New York, 2020, PP. 247-249.
166 Schroeder, Alice, *The Snowball*, Bantam Books, New York, 2008, pp. 815-819.
167 Angelo, Bob, *The NFL Off-Camera*, Temple University Press, PA, 2023, PP 208-209.
169 Jenkins, Roy, *Churchill A Biography*, Farrar, Straus & Giroux, New York, 2001, pp. 591, 819.
170 Garelick, Rhonda, *Mademoiselle*, Random House, New York, 2015, pp. 415, 418.
171 *The Magnificent Seven*, United Artists, 1960.
171 Atkins, Ann, *Golda Meir – True Grit*, Flash History Press, Paoli, PA, 2015, p. 236.
173 *Grumpy Old Men*, Warner Brothers, 1993.
175 Hainey, Michael, "Clint and Scott Eastwood," *Esquire*, August 3, 2016.
176 Carlson, Erin, *Queen Meryl*, Hachette Books, New York, 2019, p. 249.
177 *First Contact*, Ronin Films, 1983.
178 *First Contact*, Ronin Films, 1983.
179 Thoreau, Henry, *Walden*, Barnes & Noble, New York, 1993, p. 75.
180 Eyles, Carlos, *Last of the Blue Water Hunters*, Watersport Publishing, 1985, p. 32.
180 Thoreau, Henry, *Walden*, Barnes & Noble, New York, 1993, p. 266.
181 Vonnegut, Kurt, *Slaughterhouse Five*, Dial Press, New York, 2009, p. 40.
181 Shields, Charles, *And So it Goes*, Henry Holts & Co, New York, 2011, pp. 71, 149.
183 Reuters, *David Bowie's Music Catalogue Sold to Warner Music for $250M*, Jan 4, 2022.
184 Springsteen, Bruce, *Born to Run*, Simon & Schuster, New York, 2016, pp.468-469.
184 Kamp, David, *Cover Story: Bruce Springsteen*, *Vanity Fair*, September 6, 2016.
185 Finkel, Michael, "The Last True Hermit," *GQ*, August 4, 2014.

186 Finkel, Michael, "The Last True Hermit, *GQ*, August 4, 2014.

187 Hart, Michael, *The 100*, Carol Publishing, New York, 1994, pp. 341-344.

189 *The Bucket List*, Warner Brothers, 2007.

190 *The Bucket List*, Warner Brothers, 2007.

193 Musashi, Miyamoto, *A Book of Five Rings*, Overlook Press, New York, 1994, pp. 16-17, 35.

195 Goldstein, Richard, "The Shaman as Superstar," *New York Magazine*, August 5, 1968.

195 Hopkins, Jerry, "Jim Morrison Breaks Through," *Rolling Stone*, July 26, 1969.

196 *The Doors*, Elektra, 1967.

197 *Forrest Gump*, Paramount Pictures, 1995.

197 White, E.B., *Charlotte's Web*, Harper Collins, New York, 1980, pp. 94, 171.

198 White, E.B., *Charlotte's Web*, Harper Collins, New York, 1980, pp. 170, 163-164.

199 Lynn, Kenneth, *Hemingway*, Simon and Schuster, New York, 1987, pp. 429, 435.

## Bonus LIFEPATH Essays!

To receive these five additional essays for free, sign up at www.nealengstrom.com or follow the QR code.

Bonus Essay #1: Meaning of Life

Bonus Essay #2: Tapping Polynesia

Bonus Essay #3: Surfing the Tsunami

Bonus Essay #4: Befriend the Locals

Bonus Essay #5: The Two Kurts

nealengstrom.lifepath

nealengstrom

@NealEngstrom

## ABOUT THE BOOK

During the Covid pandemic, I wrote the book I would have loved to have stumbled upon during my senior year of college or received as a graduation gift. A book containing a framework for thinking about life after school, and a manual for pursuing continuous personal fulfillment.

Over the years I had filled an old cigar humidor with observational notes scribbled on cocktail napkins and scraps of paper. For one hundred days in a row during the Covid lockdown, I took a long walk and wrote a two-page essay based on those notes to create the book you hold in your hands.

Our lives consist of five stages—adventures, mission, family, tribe, legacy—each building upon one another. *YOUR LIFEPATH* contains a framework for self-discovery, and a roadmap for achieving personal fulfillment throughout each of the life stages. Fulfillment will ultimately be accomplished by figuring out what we were born to do and spending our lives doing it.

## ABOUT THE AUTHOR

Neal Engstrom is a Harvard graduate and Stanford MBA. He traveled the world and worked as a flight instructor and skydive jump pilot prior to becoming a commercial real estate professional. In 2006 he founded real estate investment firm, Engstrom Realty Fund. He and his wife of 27 years, Giselle, have raised three children and reside in Southern California.

Visit www.nealengstrom.com for more information.

- nealengstrom.lifepath
- nealengstrom
- @NealEngstrom